BACK STORY ALASKA

WRITTEN BY

LANCE BREWER

Written by Lance Brewer
Photographs by Robert Dreeszen**
Edited by Lynn Diane Smith
Proof Edit by Kathryn Kimbrel
Book design by Tyler Hartlage
Book Cover Photograph by Pete T. Barta

Back Story Alaska
www.backstoryalaska.com
Copyright © 2018 by Lance A. Brewer

ISBN (978-1-7323709-0-6)
**All photographs by Robert Dresszen unless otherwise noted

Table of Contents

BY LANCE BREWER

Introduction

IT'S THE ODDEST THING. I didn't set out to write Back Story Alaska. It happened serendipitously when I sat down one morning in February and wrote a poem. That particular morning, I woke up to discover that the outdoor skating pond where I enjoyed speedskating early in the morning was unsafe to use due to unseasonably warm weather. As I sat alone in the dark, waiting for the sun to rise, I had the thought that 'Winter Lied to Me.' So, I uncharacteristically wrote a poem about it.

The next day, my plans to go back country skiing were canceled due to lack of snow. I expressed my frustration in the form of another poem. This trade, poems for winter events, repeated itself for the following thirty days. At the end of that period I had written a total of twenty-two poems. This was odd behavior, especially since I have never written poetry before. A poetry vortex had opened.

During this same period of time, around 2:45 AM one morning, my life partner asked me, "What in the world are you doing up writing poetry in the middle of the night?" I sheepishly replied, "I have no idea." Since it seemed pointless, I put the poetry away for a few days. By day three of my respite from the poetry a voice in my head asked, "Why did you write twenty-two poems?"
In my attempt to quiet the voice, I sat down to write an explanation, 'the back story,' for each poem. At the end of fourteen days, I had married each poem to a companion back story. After the back stories were written, I realized that the poems represented a history of events that occurred during my lifetime, lessons I had learned, personal experiences I have had and the people with whom I have shared the experiences. It was at that point that I realized that this vibrant world that surrounds us is constantly trying to teach us a series of lessons.

None of us will live long enough to find the answers to all life's lessons. Some people are fortunate enough to have friends and relatives that will whisper a few of the answers. If you are lucky enough to be surrounded by those people, then you are lucky enough. I thought it would be interesting to put the collection of back stories into chronological order. As the back stories unfolded, I added the photographs that were representative of the events.

One of the personalities that you will meet in Back Story Alaska is an extraordinary individual known as 'Ugashik Bob.' He is the artist that captured the majority of the photographs you will view. Naturally, prior to publishing Back Story Alaska, I asked Ugashik Bob, and his wife Carol, to review the text and pictures. After their first reading, Ugashik Bob and Carol suggested that I convey to you that Back Story Alaska is not make believe. Although I changed some of the names to respect the privacy of others, the events contained in Back Story Alaska are experiences and adventures we shared and are sharing with you. The photographs depict Bob and Carol's interaction with bears, eagles, wolves and foxes in their natural surroundings. At their core, Bob and Carol believe that the animals that inhabit Alaska are a great gift. Their message is one of preservation and respect of wildlife in Alaska and elsewhere.

It is our sincere hope that you will fall in love with Alaska, the wildlife and people that thrive in The Great Land.

So come on, have fun, take this adventure with us.

© Ugashik Bob 2015

CHAPTER 1

Legacy and Lessons

In 1993, my father had planned and prepaid for a fishing trip to Alaska. The initial plan was for my Dad and sixteen of his colleagues to travel to a remote fishing lodge located on the Chuit Creek, which is approximately thirty-five miles west of Anchorage, Alaska. A few days before the departure date, for reasons that were never made clear to me, Dad decided that he did not want to go on the trip, but he suggested that I take his spot. He barely had the words out of his mouth, "Lance, I don't want to go to Alaska, would you -" before I accepted the offer. A ten-day trip to bush Alaska during the heart of the salmon run is an outdoorsman's dream. I was not about to let the opportunity pass me by, despite the fact that I did not know a single soul on the trip.

The trip started with an excursion around Lake Hood, the seaplane base located adjacent to the Anchorage International Airport. Lake Hood is the world's busiest seaplane base, handling an average of 190 flights per day. The base has its own control tower, and during the winter months the frozen surface of the lake is maintained for ski-equipped airplanes.

I was truly intrigued by the concept of landing an airplane on the water, and then taking off from the water. I was really disappointed when they separated us into groups of five passengers, instructing my group to take our gear to a Cessna 207. The Cessna that would be transporting our group was sitting on the dirt airstrip located adjacent to Lake Hood. Oh well, my dream of flying in a float plane would have to wait.

As we departed the Lake Hood airstrip, over flying the Cook Inlet, I marveled at the beauty of majestic Alaska. It was a clear day and we could see all the way to Denali, some 220 miles north of Anchorage, Alaska. We landed on a dirt airstrip located near the power plant in Beluga. After we landed, I turned to the gentleman sitting next to me and said, "This is one of the most amazing things I have ever done.

I am going to go home to California, learn to fly, buy a float plane and bring it back here so that I can explore Alaska." He smiled, nodded and said, "That's nice. I've been thinking about becoming an astronaut and going to the moon." Well, that joke was on him. I now have over 5000 flight hours; over 1500 hours flying floats and skis around Alaska. As for the astronaut sitting next to me on the plane that day maybe he just circled and came home, because in the past 25 years or so I haven't heard of anyone landing on the moon.

We arrived at the Chuit Creek late in the day, but during that time of year there are close to twenty-three hours of daylight which is why Alaska is referred to as the Land of the Midnight Sun. The long days are due to the earth's tilt in relation to its orbit around the sun. The earth's axis between the north and south poles is angled at 23.5 degrees away from the plane of the earth's orbit around the sun. It is bizarre to be outside at midnight under what feels like late afternoon sunshine. By the time we got settled in our bunks it was quite late. Around 10:00 PM. I made my way down to the Chuit Creek with a young fishing guide. Since he was from Texas, I will call him Tex. Tex and I engaged in the perfunctory exchange of information regarding geography, his professional life, siblings and then he shared with me that he had recently become engaged. It followed that we talked about his life in Texas, the places he had visited in Alaska and stories about fishing. Eventually, Tex used the phrase that I have heard a million times in my career: "Hey Lance, you're a lawyer, right?" The further away I am from my office or a courtroom the more likely it is that this phrase is the precursor to free legal advice. In light of the fact that I was about to spend the following ten days with this young fellow, I answered the question in the affirmative, and offered my best advice, riverside and river wise.

"I sure am," I said. "Tell me about it, Tex." Tex went on to explain that the preceding fall he had worked in southwestern Alaska as a hunting guide, shuttling caribou hunters hither and yawn. Tex was driving a small fishing skiff up the remote Ugashik River, transitioning hunters from one caribou hunting spot to another. That particular river, like most rivers in Alaska, has a multitude of twists and turns. The river is subject to the tidal influence of the ocean so the depth of the river changes twice daily. It is hard to imagine that the tide of the ocean can affect the depth of a river some thirty miles inland, but it is true. The tidal swings in Alaska are second only to the Bay of Fundy in Canada, which holds bragging rights to the highest tides in the world. The largest tides take place in an area that separates New Brunswick from Nova Scotia. At certain times of the year, the difference between high and low tide in this bay is taller than a three-story building.

Some of the highest tides in the United States are experienced near Anchorage, Alaska. In that area, the tidal flow ranges up to forty feet, or 12.2 meters. Since the shores of the Cook Inlet are flat, the shape and geometry of the coastline contribute to the effects of the tide. This can play havoc on pilots and fisherman alike. For example, a fisherman can drive his boat from an open inlet in a bay from the ocean all the way up a river in the morning. When the fisherman makes his return trip, heading downstream to the bay that same afternoon, he might find the tide has gone out. His attempt to leave the river for the ocean may be futile, since the ocean water may be as much as a mile away. If he takes the chance, he may find that his boat is sitting in just a few inches of water.

Adding to tidal woes is wind. As I start with the next explanation, it occurs to me that throughout this book I am going to talk about a village called "King Salmon." Just so that you don't confuse the village of King Salmon with the fish "King Salmon," I will refer to the fish as a "Chinook" and the village as "King Salmon." The people that are responsible for giving places a name should not be permitted to consume alcohol while doing so. Back to the tides. One such river, the Naknek River, runs east and west. On rivers like the Naknek in King Salmon, Alaska, if the wind blows out of the west, or "up" the Naknek River concurrent with the arrival of a large tide, the water level will be significantly higher. Not only does the tidal influence push the water up the river, the west wind, pushing in the same direction, will push a monumental amount of water. This increases the effects of the tide. On low tide, a person who lives on such a river will walk from a gangway located on the shoreline some sixteen feet down to the dock. Later that day, when the tide is high, that same person will walk from the shoreline on a level gangway to the same dock. The water will have risen sixteen feet. Mother Nature has moved a mountain of water.

In any event, young Tex was not particularly familiar with the subtleties and contours of the Ugashik River, the effects of the tides and the depth of the water. Earlier in the day, when Tex was transporting a caribou hunter, Tex had traversed the same spot on the Ugashik River when the tide was high. He had plenty of water under his boat, and he had no problem manipulating the boat at high speeds from the

Ugashik Lake all the way down to the lower lagoon of the Ugashik River. Unfortunately, when Tex and his fellow guide, Dick, attempted to make the return passage from the lagoon back to the mouth of the lower Ugashik Lake later in the day, Tex struck a shallow spot in the river, a sandbar, and poor old Dick took flight. He landed in the front of the skiff, his shoulder violently striking the aluminum bench seat of the skiff, dislocating his shoulder.

Tex went on to tell me that it was his good fortune that there was a doctor on the caribou hunt. In addition to the Doctor, a middle-aged man he called Bill came to Dick's aid. Tex was able to radio the base camp at his lodge, The Bear's Den. The base camp, in turn, radioed the Coast Guard located on Kodiak Island. The Coast Guard dispatched a helicopter. Dick was given a ride to Kodiak Island, Alaska. At that time, the only medical assistance available in Kodiak was a well-trained veterinarian, so Dick was medivacked to Anchorage where a doctor attended to him.

As mentioned, Tex had just popped the question to his fiancé. He was concerned that a lawsuit would be filed, and that he would lose all of his property to Dick. Tex wanted to know if he would be personally liable to Dick or would his employer be obligated to pay? He was genuinely concerned. I gave him my best guess, while reeling in what appeared to be a 35+ pound Chinook.

At the end of the ten-day trip, I made my way back to California. I would return to Alaska at the first possible opportunity. I don't know what it is about Alaska that stirs yet calms me. It seems odd to have opposite emotions, stirring versus calm, in the same person. An oxymoron. Well, not really. When you find your place, or your person, in the world, this strange excitement coexists with peace of mind.

With this newfound passion, two things needed to be taken care of immediately. First, I enrolled in flight school. Second, I developed a plan for my immediate return to Alaska that same summer. I began calling various outfitters throughout the state of Alaska. Ironically, the best source of information for lodges inside of Alaska would come from sources outside of Alaska. Go figure. I was referred to a guy in Chicago that booked fishermen in lodges throughout Alaska during the prime fishing seasons.

He told me that, historically, a large mass of sockeye salmon would next return to Alaska around July 9. The vacation guide from Chicago suggested that I travel to one of five rivers in early July to catch sockeye salmon. He suggested I select the Nushagak, Alagnak, Eggegik, Naknek or Ugashik Rivers for the best fishing, confusing names to say the least.

As I feverishly made notes of the names of the rivers I thought that he must be joking. This looks like the eye chart for the Department of Motor Vehicles! The travel guide convinced me that the largest number of sockeye salmon would return to the Ugashik River. At the time, I had no clue where to go and the names all sounded the same to me. After all, Alaska is a huge state. You could fit Texas into Alaska two times! Alaska has more than 50% of the entire U.S. coastline, or 6,640 miles and Texas only has 367 miles of coastline. As children we were shown maps of Hawaii and Alaska adjacent to one another, with the pictures of those two states set off in the lower left-hand corner of a map of the United States. The people who create maps designate a very small area to depict Hawaii and Alaska, so it is misleading for children, and apparently, adults from Texas. Most people have the mistaken impression that Alaska is a small spot in the world. Clearly, it is not.

My new friend from Chicago, whose name I have long forgotten, suggested that I call a gentleman by the name of Ted. Ted lived in Redondo Beach, California, just down the way from me. I had been told he had the inside scoop on a lodge in southwest Alaska. I called Ted. It's not hard to find the goodness in a person that will spend an hour on the telephone telling you everything he knows about Alaska. Ted gushed about Ugashik. If I was not already thrilled with anticipation, I was even more excited about returning to Alaska after talking to Ted. He suggested that I stay at the Bear's Den Lodge on the Ugashik River. Ted informed me that he would be building a cabin immediately adjacent to the Bear's Den. He was anxious for me to meet the people he was working with, Bob and Carol, and for me to fish with him in the evenings. We became fast friends.

So, my much-anticipated trip to Ugashik involves a 'Bob', a 'Carol' and a 'Ted'. Sorry to disappoint… there is no 'Alice'. Ted gave me the telephone number for the Bear's Den, which I promptly dialed. The owner of the lodge informed me that he sold the lodge to a new group of outfitters. The lodge was now known as the Ugashik River Lodge. I called the number he provided. I was initially informed that the lodge was not yet accepting guests. Disheartened, I figured that I still had four other rivers to choose from, so I started dialing for adventure. Within ten or so minutes a man that identified himself as "Richard" from the Ugashik River Lodge called me back. He told me that, although the lodge was not accepting guests, they would allow me to visit the lodge as a solo guest for a "no frills" ten-day trip from July 9 to July 19. I cheerfully accepted the invitation.

On July 8, I boarded an early morning flight from Orange County, California to Seattle; Seattle to Anchorage; Anchorage to King Salmon. It was 6 PM and I was still 75 miles north of Ugashik. I had enlisted a local floatplane pilot to take me from King Salmon to Ugashik, via floatplane, to be dropped off at the foot of the Ugashik River Lodge. I soon learned about the vagaries of flying floatplanes, weather, etc. in southwest Alaska. The float plane operator informed me that he would not be able to take me to Ugashik due to weather and other constraints. He suggested I take a flight with a commercial operator, Penn Air, to the Ugashik Village. After he made the suggestion, I walked out the back door of his small terminal and watched a group of young men load a refrigerator into a Beaver floatplane parked on his dock. I now understood the meaning of the phrase "and other constraints".

When I informed the lodge that my efforts to fly from King Salmon directly to the lodge were abandoned, they said it could be a problem since the Ugashik River Lodge is 27 miles up the Ugashik River from a dirt landing strip in the Village of Ugashik. Nevertheless, they suggested I spend the night in King Salmon, as Richard would not brave the Ugashik River in a skiff until the following morning. Richard did just that. I won't bore you with the perils of riding in a sixteen-foot skiff in high winds from the Ugashik Village to the Lower Ugashik River, but it's not for the faint of heart.

As we motored up the river, it looked as though the bottom of the river was covered with twenty- to thirty-three-inch stones. Richard would later explain that all those large dark stones were sockeye salmon, swimming from the mouth of the Ugashik River to their spawning grounds of the lower and upper Ugashik Lakes. It was hard to wipe the smile off my face, since that is exactly where we were headed. We did not arrive at the Ugashik River Lodge until late in the afternoon.

By the time I checked in, the new owners had emptied a rather large "day bottle" of whiskey and were well into day two of their supply. Richard offered me dinner, and as I ate Richard said "Lance, you have that look in your eyes. I know you saw all those fish as we motored up the river. You must be chomping at the bit to get on the river. He suggested that we go out for an hour or so and make a few casts.

We did just that. At the mouth of the Ugashik River, where the river meets the lower Ugashik Lake, there were so many fish you could, quite literally, walk across them. Richard sat on the bank of the river, watching me catch fish after fish after fish. About twenty fish into the evening, Richard uttered

that all too familiar phrase, "Hey Lance, you're a lawyer, right?"

With a knowing smile I replied, "Yes". I thought to myself that legal advice is a small price to pay for all that Richard had endured in getting me to the Lower Ugashik Lake. Richard started to tell me what sounded like a very familiar story. He explained that he had been guiding caribou hunters on this very river the year before, and that a young guide from Texas was driving a boat. The boat had... I said, "Richard, stop the story right there. If you don't mind I would like to finish it for you." Confused, he asked, "I'm sorry?" I picked it up from there: "So the story continues with the boat hitting a sandbar in the river, you flew from the back of the boat, hitting and dislocating your shoulder on the front seat of the boat. It was your good fortune that there was a doctor on the caribou hunt. He was accompanied by a middle-aged man named Bill. The elderly doctor and Bill came to your aid, and Tex was able to radio the base camp at the Bear's Den. The base camp, in turn, radioed the Coast Guard on Kodiak Island, and the Coast Guard dispatched a helicopter. You were medivacked to Kodiak and then to Anchorage. Did I miss anything?"

Dick wanted to know "how in hell" I knew about the event. I informed him that I was fishing the Chuit River in June, some 290 miles away, with a young guide by the name of Tex, from Texas, and he told me the same story. Small world?

The next morning, I walked next door to find Bob and Ted working on the roof of Bob and Carol's place. Carol invited me in for coffee, noting that she was down to her last cup of water. She explained that all their water is pumped from the river to a bladder tank under the Cabin. I noticed aloud as I walked through the yard that there is a cement slab that supports the solar panels with an imprint that reads "B & C Power Company." Carol laughed and said, "Yes, that stands for the Bob and Carol Power Company. We get all of our electricity from the solar power and wind generators."

I was naturally curious about Carol's history. Surely, she was born and raised in bush Alaska? Not so. Carol was born on April 3, 1946 in Wabasha, Minnesota. She grew up on a farm overlooking the Mississippi River and Kellogg, Minnesota. As a child, she loved "just being outdoors", and that

hasn't changed. Bob and Carol's first meeting occurred in the back seat of a friend's car (get your mind out of the gutter) when Bob and friends gave Carol a ride to church. It so happened there was a keg of beer on the seat between Bob and Carol, which was a glowing indicator of Bob's lifestyle at the time. Bob was so intimidated by Carol's beauty that he never got past "hello", as Bob tells the story, truly believing that Carol was a woman out of his reach.

Bob was and remains persistent, so they were married in Kellogg, Minnesota six months later on February 12, 1966. Before they were married, Carol had worked as a nurse's aide at St Mary's Hospital. Thereafter, she worked evenings at Michael's Steak house in Rochester, Minnesota. In early 1970, Bob and Carol moved to Sioux Falls, South Dakota, where Carol worked at a nursing home and Dinsmore, a window manufacturing company. In early 1983, Bob and Carol moved to Eagle River, Alaska where Carol started her own cleaning business. During that time, Bob was employed by IBM, which required that he travel the world. So, Carol accompanied Bob to Venezuela, the Philippines and many large, urban quagmires of the United States.

In May of 1986, the first wing of their home in Ugashik went up. From that point in time on, Carol was deeply involved in the never-ending project. Clearly, Bob was blessed with a mate that wanted to take on the challenge of building a home in bush Alaska. What a leap of faith! Carol remained strong in her conviction to live in bush Alaska, even during the periods that frustrated Bob, while he was considering other options. As I stood in front of Bob and Carol's place, I found it difficult to imagine the blood, sweat and tears involved in the years they spent building their home.

In addition to the house, they constructed a twenty-foot by fifteen-foot solar panel. The solar panel includes a tracking device that causes the panel to rotate as the solar panel follows the sun across the horizon. Bob and Carol poured the foundation which holds the solar panels in place by hand. Since the famous winds of Ugashik would likely take the panels away like a kite in the wind, Bob and Carol poured 3600 pounds of concrete in the base. In true pioneer style, Bob and Carol hand-carried forty bags of concrete, each weighing 90 pounds, to the site of their solar panels. To provide minutiae on building in the bush, each bag of concrete had to be shipped from Anchorage, some 360 miles away, to the Ugashik Village. Once the concrete reached the village, the concrete was off-loaded by hand. When the weather permitted, Bob and/or Carol were required to drive their sixteen-foot boat (more appropriately "skiff") some twenty-seven miles down the river, always potentially treacherous depending on the winds that particular day. When Bob and/or Carol reached the village, depending on the tide, they carried the bags of concrete some 10 to 30 yards down to the skiff to be transported twenty-seven miles back up the river to their home at the lower Ugashik Lakes. Once they arrived home, to use a 'Bobism,' they "humped" the bags of concrete up the 25-foot bank to its new home in Ugashik. A Bobism is a quote, saying, or words of wisdom from Ugashik Bob, of which I will use many herein. Back to transporting items from the Ugashik Village to Bob and Carol's house. I used the concrete as an example. The process of retrieving, transporting and unloading of goods at Bob and Carol's house applies to everything from a pack of matches to a kitchen table. Everything that comes in and out of Ugashik must make the trip from the village, some twenty-seven miles, to the Lower Ugashik Lake. Everything. I once had a coach ask me during an intense work out, "Who is more committed, the chicken that lays the egg or the pig that gives the meat?" Bob and Carol definitely "give the meat" - they are 100% committed.

If you get the feeling that Ugashik Bob and Carol are two tenacious individuals, go with the feeling. Ugashik Bob joined the Navy in June of 1961. Bob would politely say that he joined the Navy to escape a small town in southwest Minnesota. If you're lucky enough to spend eleven minutes with Bob, you come away with the impression that Bob was more than mischievous as a teenager. Hence, the keg of beer on the back seat of the car when he met Carol. Clearly, the Navy was the better of two options for a young man with his intellect and energy. During my visit, I volunteered to help Bob carry a stack of 2 x 4's from the river's edge, up the bank to the back of his property. I grabbed a couple of 2 x 4's. Bob grabbed four. We repeated the back and forth process of unloading wood for an hour but on one trip, as Bob made his way up the bank of the river, he stumbled and fell. Before he hit the ground, Bob shouted in an odd voice, presumably that of his father, "Get up! You're not hurt!"

There is only one attribute about Bob that exceeds his tenacity and toughness, and that's his intelligence. After being tested extensively by the Navy, he was among a select few to serve as an Aviation Electricians Mate. Bob tells some great stories about flying on and off aircraft carriers. Bob began his career with IBM, in Rochester, Minnesota, as a Senior Large Systems Engineer. Yes, he is, and definitely remains, a "brainiac." In February of 1983, Bob was transferred to Anchorage. Mind you, this was not an involuntary transfer. Bob spent most of his adult life hunting and fishing. Alaska is the dream of any outdoorsman, especially a man like Bob, and he has the trophies to prove it. In September of 1985, Bob went on a fishing trip to the Ugashik Narrows. It was love at first bite - I totally understand. Bob absolutely had to find a plot of land upon which to build he and Carol a home. It is difficult to find private land for sale in the area in and around the Ugashik Lake. The majority of the land is National Park Land or land that is controlled by the Bureau of Land Management. Also, several refuges surround Bob and Carol's place. Bob persevered and found one of the few patches of public land available for purchase in the immediate area. Six months later, in May of 1986, he and Carol started building their home.

Sometime around 1989, Ted was visiting the Bear's Den Lodge and he met Bob and Carol. Like most people, he fell in love with them. For the following five years, Ted was active in helping Bob and Carol build their home. Bob and Carol moved to Ugashik as full-time residents in May of 1996. With the exception of a couple of winters in Costa Rica, they have been full time residents through the winter of 2016/2017. The concept of living as the only full-time residents in Ugashik, Alaska is daunting. A discussion for another day.

The balance of my time in Ugashik was spent fishing by day and trading stories with Bob, Carol and Ted at night. I guess I had become Alice. You might have a vision of four of us eating out of a can of Spam, but this is not a scene from "A Man, A Can and A Microwave." Truth be known, Carol would put Martha Stewart to shame. Despite the fact that the Ugashik River Lodge included meals with my stay at the lodge, I would drop in first thing in the morning. Carol would place a stack of French toast, stuffed with cream cheese on the table. I, in turn, would proclaim "No thank you, I've already eaten." Bob retorted, "I dare you, Lance. I'll bet you can't eat just one. They're like Lay's potato chips. Good luck." With each passing day I had become more impressed with Bob and Carol's accomplishments. From home construction, electronics, wind generators, solar panels, computers, radio phones, satellite Internet service, to smoked salmon, baking and food fit for a five-star restaurant. You name it, they cooked or engineered it, and did it inexplicably well.

The following is an expression of my early impressions of Bob and Carol. I hope you will keep an open mind to a different form of expression, a poem. Each chapter of Back Story Alaska will culminate in a poem summarizing the chapter.

LEGACY AND LESSONS

My father yelled — "come on squirt"
"Get up — you're not hurt"
I was born — in a different age,
No soft landings — to assuage

My generation — failed to create
A legacy — make your own fate
Desperate for solutions — running out of time
So many lessons — as the bell chimes

Words of wisdom — before I go
Don't be a victim — a patsy-scarecrow
Sing for your dinner — never be late
Take care of your family — control your own fate

You're the man — take the lead,
Never let love — be driven by need
Work real hard — imagine more
In your relationships — don't keep score

Legacy is built — on the slow
Over generations — like glacial snow
It's all just — a matter of pride
You have legacy — on your side

© Ugashik Bob 2015

CHAPTER 2

Ludwig, Oh Mighty Bear

BY AND BY, I returned home to California where I continued my quest to secure a pilot's license. The chill of fall was in the air. That may sound romantic, but I do live in California, so I may have gotten a little carried away. But, we do have duck hunting in Southern California. I was fortunate enough to secure a blind at a private hunting club behind Prado Dam in Chino, California. I called my young nephew, Courtney, and informed him that I had reserved him a spot to go duck hunting on opening day. I asked Courtney if he had completed his hunter safety course and he gleefully informed me that he had. He was ready to hunt.

Shortly after hanging up the telephone with Courtney the phone rang and it was him again. He asked if it would be okay for his friend Patrick to join us on opening day of the duck hunting season. As any good uncle would do, I gave a resounding "Yes! But only if Patrick has also completed his hunter safety course." Courtney confirmed Patrick had his hunter safety card. In the background, an excited Patrick exclaimed his excitement at joining us on opening day of duck hunting season.

I hung up the phone with the comfort that I had made two young boys happy. Within minutes, the telephone rang again. It was Courtney. He was now inquiring whether there was room in the duck blind for Patrick's father, Bill. I said, "Of course. There's always room for one more."

The opening day of duck hunting season arrived with a bang - literally. The boys did a great job calling and shooting ducks. Our dog, Sarah, frolicked on her retrieves, as a young dog will do. A good time was being had by all. The conversation between the new acquaintances began with Bill asking me, "What other outdoor activities do you enjoy?" I explained to him that I had just taken my check-ride to become a private pilot. The next step for me would be to get my seaplane rating. I explained that I made a couple of trips to Alaska the preceding summer. "I think this place, Alaska, is my new passion. I am going to spend time, next summer, exploring Alaska in a floatplane." When I mentioned "Ugashik", Bill interrupted me.

Bill said, "That's crazy, I just took a trip to Ugashik, Alaska a year ago this fall. The strangest thing happened. My friend, Dr. Ed, and I were on a caribou hunt..." I almost lost my mind! Was I really hearing "Ugashik, Dr. Ed, Bill, caribou hunt, Alaska? " In a nano-second all the adrenaline in my body rushed to my head as I realized I had just won the story lottery!

"Bill!" I exclaimed, "Stop right there! Let ME finish the story!" That was not a very respectful way to treat my new friend, but excitement reigned, so I continued. "Tex was guiding a group of caribou hunters, which includes you and Dr. Ed. Tex, your caribou hunting guide, was transitioning from one hunting spot to another, on his way from the lagoon on the Ugashik River to the lower Ugashik Lake. Tex was driving the boat. Dick, another guide, was in the back of the boat when Tex managed to run the boat into a shallow spit. Dick flew into the front of the boat, dislocating his shoulder. It was his good fortune that your friend, Dr. Ed, was on the caribou hunt. You and Dr. Ed came to Dick's aid, and Tex was able to get word to the Coast Guard on Kodiak Island. The Coast Guard dispatched a helicopter and Dick was saved."

Bill was stupefied, as was I. "How in the world did you hear that story?" I said, "You don't know the half of it!" I have heard that story, not once, not twice, but three times, at three different locations! Your caribou guide, Tex, first told me the story in June on the Chuit River. A month or so later, some three hundred miles away, Dick told me the story on my visit to Ugashik, at what used to be the Bear's Den. And now, three months and 3600 miles away, you are telling the exact same story. What are the odds?"

And so began the surreal experiences I would have in and around Alaska. Within a month I had completed the process of getting a seaplane rating. I returned to Alaska, and as promised, I purchased a floatplane. My friend Rick, who I will call "Racer", took the plane off floats, converting it to a wheel plane. The floats would spend the early part of their existence on Lake Hood. That winter Racer and I flew the plane, affectionately called "Juliet Yankee", back to California so that I could garner the much-needed flight experience in anticipation of my return with Juliet Yankee to Alaska.

In May of the following year, Racer and I flew Juliet Yankee back to Alaska so the plane could again be converted to a floatplane. We returned to America (well, it felt like a different country) for a few weeks while the aviation maintenance professionals converted Juliet Yankee from a wheel plane, back to a floatplane. I returned to Alaska in June. I hired a flight instructor to fly with me from Anchorage, through the Lake Clark Pass, and down the Alaska Peninsula to Ugashik. The goal of the trip was two-fold. First, I needed to satisfy the insurance company by completing the requisite flight time 'on floats.' I think, at the time, the insurance company wanted me to fly ten hours, in Alaska, with an instructor. Truthfully, ten hours of flight time in a floatplane, in Alaska, is nothing. It's meaningless. A pilot who has logged one-hundred hours of flight time in Alaska is, relatively speaking, an infant bush pilot. So green that they don't even know what they don't know. But I had satisfied the requirements of the insurance company by

completing the requisite number of flight hours. After a flurry of take offs and landings the flight instructor left me in King Salmon. He would return to 'Los Anchorage', another Ugashik Bobism, taking a commercial airline flight out of King Salmon, back to the 'Big Village', aka Anchorage.

I was now on my own. As I made my first solo flight in Alaska, on floats, it was daunting. I lined up for my first solo landing over a large lake. Something did not seem quite right. It then occurred to me that I had no one to talk to. There was complete silence. I had completed all my training in and around big city airports, with control towers. It was a mixed blessing. My training prepared me to be a somewhat competent pilot in busy airspace. In that environment, there is constant radio chatter. But here, there was no control tower. No air traffic controllers. No one to talk to. Add to that, no flight instructor. More silence. It was surreal.

I completed three solo touch and goes, or in float plane vernacular, 'splash and goes,' and decided it was time to begin my life as a real float plane pilot. I was heading down to Ugashik to see my friends Bob and Carol at their place on the lower Ugashik Lake and mouth of the Ugashik River. There would be one stop. The famous Ugashik Narrows. This is the site of the state record grayling. I had to land and fish the Narrows, a rite of passage. It was only a ten-minute flight from the Narrows to Bob and Carol's place. After all, I only had to survive one take-off and landing in the Narrows.

It was a day I will never forget. I was feeling both the fear and bewilderment about having traveled to what then seemed like such a remote place. As is typical in Alaska, the weather changed. It was a rainy, windy day in the Ugashik Narrows. After safely landing in the Narrows, I unwittingly taxied Ju-

liet Yankee cross wind and cross current, barely making it to the opposite shoreline. While I was struggling to get Juliet Yankee out of the river's current and tied down, a voice with a heavy German accent seemingly came from nowhere beckoning "Hallo, my name is Ludwig, what is your name?" I attempted a response, but Ludwig's follow up inquiry came so quickly. "Why did you fly to the Narrows on such an awful day?" I provided a brief explanation.

Ludwig then generously directed me to an area of the Narrows where he thought I might have the best chance to find grayling and char. He suggested that I catch a few fish and then walk a few hundred meters up to his cabin to have a cup of hot coffee with him and "Susan".

I was truly intrigued by my newfound friend and the concept that his Susan had apparently decided to trade a summer in the comforts of cosmopolitan Germany for the remoteness that is Ugashik, Alaska.

After I caught a few fish, I made my way up to the cabin to have coffee with Ludwig and Susan. As I approached, I recognized that the cabin did not have running water, electricity, indoor plumbing or other such amenities. I thought that "Susan" must be quite a woman. As I entered the cabin, Ludwig had only two cups of hot coffee sitting on the table. I was confused so I asked Ludwig, "No coffee for Susan?" Ludwig explained that "'Susan did not drink coffee."

By and by, Ludwig and I sat for a bit, drinking coffee and exchanging stories of what brought us to Alaska, and specifically, the Narrows. When Ludwig spoke of the Narrows, his voice cradled it like something of great value.

Ludwig went on to explain that when he originally bought the cabin on the Narrows, a scoundrel that did not actually have title to the land had swindled him. Unbeknownst to Ludwig, the cabin was located in the Becharoff National Wildlife Refuge. As a result, the Department of Fish & Wildlife was in the process of evicting Ludwig from the Narrows. Ludwig explained that the dispute was ongoing, and he would be allowed to stay in the cabin for an uncertain period of time. After a long discussion about fishing, hiking and all things Alaska, I asked Ludwig when Susan would be joining us.

Ludwig looked at me, tongue in cheek, and pointing to the wall, he proclaimed, "Susan is right there." Ludwig pointed to the poster hanging on the wall next to the dining table. It was a picture of a lovely swimsuit model, Ludwig's "Susan." He explained that he and Susan got together here in Alaska in 1986. Ludwig gloated about how Susan loved being with an older man, saying that, "Susan loves my cemetery blonde hair." We both laughed about Susan's choice of men and her choice of geography.

I asked Ludwig, "How do you spend your time here at the Narrows? What do you do?" Ludwig explained that he reads on rainy days, fishes in the evenings and spends the nice days hiking. He shared stories of the numerous places he had hiked in the region. We talked, very vaguely of course, about the best fishing spots. I asked Ludwig about his longest hike. He told me that he hiked from the Ugashik Narrows to the "Pacific side."

To provide context, in order to understand this solo hike by a then-74-year-old man, you have to understand the geography of the area. Ludwig resides between the Upper Ugashik Lake and the Lower Ugashik Lake, on the Alaska Peninsula. In that location, the Alaska Peninsula is roughly thirty-seven miles wide. The Bering Sea is on one side, the Pacific Ocean or "the Pacific side" is on the other. As a crow flies, the Ugashik Narrows is roughly 20 miles from the Bering Sea. But Ludwig would hike in the opposite direction to the Pacific side. If Ludwig were flying, and he was definitely not flying, the solo trek from Ludwig's cabin on the

Bering Sea side, over to the Pacific side is roughly 17 miles across very unforgiving terrain. The only trails between the Bering Sea side and the Pacific side are trails that were created by animals. No man or woman uses those trails, save one, that I know of. The best, most frequented trails are created by brown bears — literally hundreds of brown bears. The bears encountered by Ludwig in the area of the Narrows, all the way to the Pacific side are brown bears. Just to be clear, there are no black bears in southwest Alaska. Black bears are much smaller bears, so they cannot compete with brown bears. In addition, the geography around King Salmon, including the Alaska Peninsula, consists of tundra. Black bears prefer forests to tundra. Most people who visit the Alaska Peninsula refer to the bears in the area as grizzly bears. While all grizzly bears are brown bears, not all brown bears are grizzly bears. The difference is simple. Brown bears have access to coastal food resources, such as wild Alaskan salmon, and grizzly bears live further inland. Grizzly bears typically do not have access to a marine diet.

A large male brown bear can routinely weigh over a thousand pounds. By comparison, the grizzly bears in Yellowstone National Park weigh far less on average, with the largest bear in Yellowstone weighing a maximum of nine-hundred pounds. Oh sure, ask Siri.

I asked Ludwig about his closest encounter with a brown bear. Ludwig explained that when he was on his seventeen-mile trek from the Narrows to the Pacific side, as he moved up the trail on a long, gradual slope, he looked up just in time to see an extremely large brown bear lumbering towards him. Thick alders surrounded Ludwig so he had nowhere to go. Ludwig had just enough time to draw his gun, but he quickly calculated the time and distance to the bear and realized that even if he got a shot off the bear would maul him in an instant. Ludwig would die in any event. So, Ludwig did the honorable thing. He just turned around, hugged his revolver to his chest and waited for the bear to maul him to death. Despite a brown bear's enormous size they are extremely fast, having been clocked at speeds of thirty miles per hour. It would be a matter of seconds for the bear to get to Ludwig. Ludwig waited. Not a sound. Should he move? No, the bear is just right there. The bear may be having second thoughts. If Ludwig moved, the bear would interpret his movement as an act of aggression and the stay of execution would be lifted. Ludwig waited. After a minute, Ludwig turned around. No bear.

Over the past twenty-five years, we have shared the trails and fishing spots with the brown bears of Alaska. It is always a dilemma: which way to go; give ground, don't give ground; leave the trail into the grass, stay on the trail and retreat; is this a sow with cubs or a young male that can be pushed off the trail; is this bear old and sick; am I close to his or her food cache; am I upwind or downwind of this bear; does he or she smell me; what would the bear like me to do; should we trade places; let's negotiate.

And then the bear processes, attempts to makes its decision, as time flows oh so slowly - like sand through an hourglass, his mind churns. The seesaw begins. His body lumbers. All of these things enter your mind as you make, even the most casual walk, in Alaska.

I am often visited by my thoughts of Ludwig, mostly alone, on that trail from the Narrows to the Pacific side. Over the years, we have had several encounters with brown bears. Not as daunting as Ludwig's experience. This poem is a combination of my thoughts about our own experiences, coupled with the potential surreal outcome that could have visited Ludwig.

OH MIGHTY BEAR

Oh mighty Bear — so massive, so strong
We want the same thing — to just get along
You're looking for food — I look to pass
Please allow me — a detour in grass

I saw some Salmon — just down the way
A place where Bears — gorge them all day
The next move is yours — don't make me choose
— I have this weapon — I hate to use

Temper your anger — no need to rake
Lets end this 'see-saw' — it's a give and take
A burdensome message — to deliver one day
Just outside this village — two bodies decay

Your den is waiting — your winter will halt
So much to lose — with a brutal assault
Our eyes needn't meet — you can just shrug
Deep in the grass — I will trudge

With honor we've crossed — along this path
So thankful we'll never know — each other's wrath

CHAPTER 3

I Want My Problems Back

EVERY TRIP TO UGASHIK included an invitation from me to one of my three brothers to come to Alaska. If one of my brothers is not able to make the trip, I would invite close friends or family to come for the experience. One of the earliest invitations was extended to my Uncle, UB2, which he readily accepted. To UB2, "fishin' is the mission." In point of fact, "UB2" as Ugashik Bob has nicknamed him, has made the trip to Alaska with me every summer since 1994.

UB2 was born in Los Angeles, California in 1961. Ironically, UB2 is two years younger than me. My Aunt Clarissa, or Auntie Cleo as we called her, met UB2 when he was twelve years old. They stayed friends through UB2's teenage years. I would see UB2, intermittently, in the early years. UB2 met his first bride when he was in his early twenties. I lost contact with him during that time. He was happily married for a year, but actually married for five.

Shortly thereafter, Auntie Cleo approached me and asked me how I felt about her dating a younger man. Auntie Cleo is a vivacious woman with the keenest and most wicked-fast sense of humor. If you asked Auntie Cleo a stupid question, she capably responded with a very funny, often sarcastic, comment before you were able to put a question mark on the sentence. Wit and beauty were the bait, UB2 took it all 'hook, line and sinker.'

In the years that followed, when we built Camp Brewer, UB2 became the unofficial Director of Camp Maintenance and Knower of All Things Mechanical around Camp Brewer. Although I think of Alaska as the place "where you can fish all day, with only your thoughts as company", truth be told, during the early years in Alaska, I would be "fishing all day, with only UB2 as company." UB2 and I have spent hundreds of hours flying and fishing together. Over the years, as we have grown into men, and you would hope that we would act more like men. But in our silly times together we still engage in childish endeavors, like making up our own words and phrases. It sounds funny I know, but I think old people should invent reasons to laugh, daily. This kind of silly behavior could be the fountain of

youth - the kind of thing that reverses aging or at least slows down the aging process. UB2 had become such an important part of my life that when he and Auntie Cleo got divorced in 2011, there would be no custody battle. I was able to secure full custody of UB2. Thankfully, with my Auntie Cleo's blessing.

One of my earliest memories involving UB2 happened before we built Camp Brewer. I had finished my first one-way trip to Ugashik as a solo floatplane pilot, and my next mission was a return trip to King Salmon to pick up UB2. UB2 was scheduled to arrive on a commercial flight into King Salmon around 5PM. Since I was flying to King Salmon on floats, I would have to land on the Naknek River adjacent to the commercial airport. From there, I would hike a half mile up the road to the airport to retrieve UB2 and his gear. Unfortunately, I did not have any place to park the floatplane, so I asked a local commercial floatplane pilot, Cecil Shuman, if I could park my floatplane on his dock for an hour or so. Cecil said, "No problem, I probably won't be back from the Pacific side until 8 PM or so. You will have the dock to yourself." I landed on the Naknek River without incident and taxied the floatplane towards the dock at CAir. As I approached the dock, I was relieved that the wind was completely calm. My floatplane training did not include docking a floatplane on a river. The flow of the Naknek River added a new element of difficulty. In addition, because of the tidal influence, the Naknek River would sometimes cause the river to flow backwards. In other words, the river flows towards the ocean, from east to west during part of the day. When the tide changes, during high tide, the river flows in the opposite direction, from west to east during the ocean's high tide. All of my training took place on a lake. The only time I approached a dock during training was on a calm lake, not a flowing river. Even on a lake, I made the mistake of approaching the dock with too much speed. During training I only messed up the docking 11 out of 10 times (I know).

In any event, this was the perfect evening. The wind was calm. The river's flow was as it should be, from upstream to downstream, east to west, towards the ocean. That is to say, the river was flowing as a river should, downriver. With the calm wind and the river flowing east to west, I could slowly taxi to Cecil's dock, cut the engine, step out onto the float of the floatplane, step onto the dock and tie up the plane. Easy-peasy. As I taxied up to the dock, a couple of fisherman in 16-foot fishing skiffs decided to troll in front of the float plane. One of the two boats hooked into what appeared to be a very nice salmon. Although I was taxing the float plane directly towards the dock, I was slightly distracted from my course to the dock, fearing I might get tangled up in the fishing line. As I turned the float plane away from the dock, the current of the river forced me to the center of the stream, away from the dock. I eventually got the plane turned back towards the dock. As I gathered my composure, I discovered that Cecil had already returned to King Salmon. He had parked his float plane on the front half of the dock, leaving me just enough room to put my plane on the back half of the dock. Panic set in. I realized I would have to approach the dock, calculate the speed of the airplane compared to the flow of the river such that if I chopped the power on the plane just shy of the dock I would have enough inertia to coast to the dock. Ultimately, I would need to have enough speed to make it to the dock, but not so much speed that I would be unable to stop my float plane before floating into Cecil's shiny Cessna 185. Since a floatplane pilot uses his feet to control water rudders which steer the plane in the water, my hands were free to pray that Cecil was nearby and would come down to the dock to rescue me by stopping my plane before it hit his plane.

As luck would have it, bad luck that is, no Cecil. Keep in mind, when a floatplane is in the water, it is more of a boat than a plane. Except, I have twenty feet of wingspan to contend with. As I approached the dock my fear of hitting Cecil's plane grew larger with every inch of river I traveled. As I got within twenty feet of the dock I killed the power to the plane. With no power from the engine, I continued my uncontrolled slide towards the dock and the tail of Cecil's plane. Everything was looking really good as I stepped out on the float and grabbed the rope from the front of my floats, readying myself to get close enough to the dock so that I could quickly wrap the rope around the first available cleat on the dock. As I got within six feet of the dock, I was pleased that I had just enough energy left in the slide to get the plane to the dock, but not so much that I could not arrest the plane or stop it before the front of my plane would hit the tail feathers of Cecil's plane. There I was, feeling pretty manly, standing there on a float plane in my hip waders, in Alaska. Suddenly a gust of wind came seemingly from nowhere, pushing my plane away from the dock. I had no choice. There was no way, if I could prevent it, that I was going to allow my first solo-docking of a floatplane to include damage to another airplane. All I could think about was the fact that, aside from loss of pride, Cecil would be without an airplane during the four most productive months, financially speaking, of the year. These are literally the only months of the year that a commercial pilot can make money. If I damaged his floatplane, Cecil was 'a duck out of water.' I did the only thing I could do. I leaped into the water with the rope that was secured to the float of my plane in my right hand. With my left hand, I reached for the cleat on dock. I was able to grab the cleat. The temperature of the water was such that I had no problem getting out of the river and back onto the dock.

I tied the rope around the cleat, safely securing my plane to the dock. Crisis averted. The next order of business was a matter of pride. I looked around feverishly to determine whether or not any of those fishermen had witnessed the event. Luckily for me, each boat was preoccupied with the ominous task of netting a salmon. Fantastic. Ugashik Bob is famous for saying "I should get up in the morning, have a cup of coffee, put on my hip waders, and go jump in the water and get it over with. By the end of the day I am going to be soaking wet anyway!" Now I understand. I did my best to empty my hip waders of the excess water. I sloshed my way up to the airport in King Salmon. Apparently, UB2's flight was either cancelled or delayed. This was in an age before cell phones, so I had to take a few hundred more squishy steps next door to the bar at the King Ko (not a copy store) to borrow their telephone.

As I walked into the bar at the King Ko, there were six or so locals sitting at the bar making their play for two ladies sitting at the bar. There were a couple of fellas, in the on-deck circle, playing a game of pool. The presence of two attractive women is no small event. The boys, including the bartender, did not want to waste their time on me. It is common knowledge in King Salmon that "you don't lose your girl, you only lose your turn." No one in the bar could afford the distraction of a rat-soaked-city-slicker. Struggling to get the attention of the bartender, I sat at the end of the bar, sufficiently ignored. After the appropriate amount of time had passed, I politely beckoned to the bartender, "Excuse me sir, do you mind if I use your telephone to make a calling card call?" The bartender whirled around and yelled, "Sure, buddy." I have spent the majority of my adult life keenly listening between the lines. I have listened for unspoken messages being conveyed by countless lawyers, judges and witnesses. You learn to listen for a tone or gesture that is not consistent with a facial expression. As the bartender said, "Sure, buddy," he had an over-confident smirk on his face. I thought, "Here it comes…" "Hey, aren't you the lawyer from Los Angeles that just went for a swim in the Naknek? You know, you were in a no swimming zone down there by the commercial floatplane dock? Don't you know it's pretty dangerous to swim around floatplanes?!!" The laughter erupted.

That day I realized I was a labrador in wolf country. Some of the locals would prove to be territorial. Unaccepting. Like a pack of wolves, they would lie in wait for my inattentiveness, waiting for the moment that I would make a mistake. I understood. I was a city dog,
a labrador, in the presence of wolves. And when a labrador encounters a wolf, or a pack of wolves, it is bound to get eaten. I realized that day that no matter what I did the wolves were waiting, watching with pleasure, hoping for a mistake.

I would spend the following five seasons visiting Bob and Carol. After each trip to Ugashik, I would come home to proclaim to my family and friends that I had "found the land of milk and honey." I did not want to wear out my welcome at Bob and Carol's. In 1998, I decided it was time to build my own place, so I could share Alaska with friends and family. Initially each family member or friend would come, fall in love, and bring another friend or family member. The guest list grew exponentially.

One of my most memorable days in Alaska was the first day that my brother, Michael, visited Camp Brewer. This is not to say that the visits by my other relatives were any less memorable. Michael must have arrived the day that Noah stopped in Alaska to unload the Ark. Soon after Michael arrived, we climbed into the float plane. The 'mission was fishin.' We were headed to Portage Creek to do some fishing for Chinook. We followed the Naknek River to the opening of the Kvichak (pronounced Kwe-jack) Bay. It was a completely calm day. The water in the bay was smooth, which would allow for an emergency landing on the water in the event of an engine failure. We safely flew directly across the bay, over the open water, towards Portage Creek, on the Nushagak River. As we arrived mid-channel on the Kvichak Bay, Michael peered out the window of the float plane to see hundreds of beluga whales surfacing in the water below. Since the tide was changing, the water is slightly brown in tone, with the white backs of the whales surfacing, appearing as if they were floating hard-boiled eggs in the water. Michael could not believe his eyes. I could not believe my eyes. I have had the

good fortune to see a similar event, but not in the volume that Michael enjoyed. I explained to Michael that seeing that much wildlife all at once was something that he would probably not see again in his lifetime.

As we crossed the shoreline on the opposite side of the Kvichak Bay, Michael glowed as we talked about having been a witness to such an event. As we flew over the open tundra on the opposite side of the bay, we approached an incline, a ridgeline, which meanders north towards the Nushagak River. Michael spied a few caribou standing on the ridgeline. He was excited, still riding the rush of having seen all the beluga whales. I turned the plane to the north to follow the ridgeline to give Michael a better view. As I made the turn, Michael said, "There are even more along this portion of the ridge." We continued along the same track. As the flight progressed, more and more caribou came into view. We flew on for another five minutes. For the entirety of that portion of the flight we continuously spied caribou. There were thousands of them. Lightning struck twice.

We landed at Portage Creek on the Nushagak River, parked the plane, jumped in the boat and headed up the river with a burning desire for Michael to catch his first chinook. We turned off the engine to the boat. The boat was now perpendicular to the edge of the river as we quietly drifted in the river's current about ten yards off the shoreline. Typically, salmon will swim close to the shoreline. Chinook will swim deeper in the water than other types of salmon. As a result, all of the bait used to catch Chinook are designed to sink or dive to the bottom of the river. Michael was positioned perfectly. His rod tip dipped once, twice, then whack, game on. He spent the next ten minutes wrestling in a thirty-pound chinook. It was like being a kid again, brother having fun with brother.

After Michael landed the fish, we continued to drift. Michael gestured to me, whispering, "Paddle us away from the shore - there's a moose and her calves standing in the river." Sure enough, a post-card Alaskan moose was standing fifty yards down river from us with her two calves. The path of our drift, if left unabated, would take us directly in front of the moose. We quietly paddled to the center of the river. Moose can be very dangerous. Moose are territorial. They don't want anyone in their space. The locals have taught me that "you hold for a bear, but you run from a moose." On my first trip to Alaska, while fishing on the Chuit River, a man approached me. We will call him Mr. Moose. He used the familiar phrase, "I understand you're a lawyer?" He introduced himself, gesturing, he told me he lived in the cabin on the bluff, overlooking the

river. Mr. Moose pointed to a cabin which had large antenna protruding from the adjacent outbuilding. I said, "Yes I am." As we both looked towards his cabin, I inquired, "Is that antenna for a radio-telephone?" Cell phones did not exist in those days. Even if they did, there were no cell towers in that part of Alaska. The only options for communicating with the outside world were satellite telephones or radio-telephones. I had been in Alaska for seven days without having communicated with my young son, Chapman. It bothered me. It must have been troubling to my young son to be away from his father for an extended period of time. I anticipated the question to follow from Mr. Moose, "Do you have time to answer a few questions?" I replied, "Sure, we can talk about it on the way to your coffee maker and radio-telephone. Fair trade?" With ambivalence he replied, "Not a problem. Let's walk."

We traipsed up the unmade road leading to Mr. Moose's cabin. The road consisted of grainy dirt, no gravel, water had flowed through the center during a recent storm, creating a gorge down the middle of the road. Thick alders bordered the road. It was a clear, warm day. The bugs were out. Thousands of them. Mostly mosquitoes. I was completely covered in mosquito netting, with a hoodie that covered my face. I call it an "Alaskan Burqa." Mr. Moose was wearing only a golf T-shirt. I call it a golf T-shirt because it was a T-shirt with 18 holes in it. He was an unshaven, scruffy, overweight Alaskan who obviously had not taken a bath in a while. This was a remote location. There was no need or desire to dress to impress. But his attire was on the fringe of being uncivilized. As we walked, Mr. Moose ex-

plained his problems to me. The event had all happened the year before when he was cutting timber in back of his place. He was gathering deadwood, "so as to stock his wood stove for the winter." As he walked from the thickness of the alders into a small clearing behind his house, he encountered a moose. The moose, accompanied by her calf, immediately reared up, continually pummeling him with her front hooves until he was unconscious. He had the scars to prove it. It was hard to look at his injuries. Mr. Moose would be the first Alaskan to tell me "you know, you run from a moose but you hold for a bear." The point is, you don't run from a bear because, in the mind of a bear, food runs. Better to be in the mind of a bear than in his stomach, I'd say. Mr. Moose spent the following six months in a hospital in Anchorage. Suffice it to say, Mr. Moose had legal questions relating to his different options, public assistance, homestead exemptions, bankruptcy, etc. Since I am not licensed to practice law in Alaska, we could only speak in generalities. But, I told him I would send him the name of an attorney in Anchorage that would give him proper legal advice.

So, Michael and I are now understandably floating a fair distance from the moose and her calf. As we drift back towards the shoreline of the river, Michael is dragging his salmon bait on the bottom of the river, whack, another fish. As the oversized salmon leaps out of the water, my brother is beside himself. The following hour we drifted, saw another moose, and caught our fair share of fish. I swear the local Chamber of Commerce must have been queuing up wildlife for my brother. There are times in life when you can only dream of certain events or people - fantasy is better than reality. Michael's first day in Alaska does not fall into that category.

When we returned to Camp Brewer, I overheard a telephone call in which an over exuberant Michael told his bride that "we have to get the boys up here to Alaska." Michael has four sons. In high school, his classmates voted Michael 'Mostly likely to Conceive'. Three of his four sons are consistent visitors at Camp Brewer. They, in turn, bring a friend or two.

Michael had the day of days when it comes to seeing wildlife. I don't want to mislead you. You could put all of the people who have visited Camp Brewer in a room and allow them to tell their stories, which would be accompanied by their pictures of the wildlife they have seen while visiting Alaska. If you combined all of those stories, collectively, all the Campers who have visited Camp Brewer over the past twenty years have seen less wildlife than Michael saw that one day. No word of a lie. Taking into account the fishing and wildlife, it's no wonder that Michael was hooked. He would return to Alaska with gusto, that August, with his boys in tow. My nephews, and several of their friends, caught a monumental amount of fish in Eggegik that year. They went home very happy boys.

When fall arrives in Alaska, it's Mother Nature's way of sending a warning that the fun is about to end. It is as if you are in the second grade, having the time of your life at recess, when the bell rings interrupting the joy of the moment. Time to return to class for a science project. The cure for insomnia. With the arrival of fall, the chore of shutting down camp begins. One such chore is boat storage. When people from down in America think of boat storage, a vision that probably comes to mind is a boat being hauled into a marina, removed with a crane or driven up a concrete boat ramp, and placed in a fenced yard or boathouse.

The Alaska version of boat storage is slightly different. You travel a great distance to an unnamed lagoon or creek, remove the outboard engine, remove the anchor, and drag the boat as far up into the tundra as possible. In my experience, the grunting actually does get the boat about three feet further from the water. You then roll the boat over on its back, sliding the oars of the boat under the boat for winter storage. As you roll the boat over on its back, you check the area to ensure you do not place the boat over an open hole, which may serve as entrance and exit to a den used by small animals. If you do cover such an access point, you have just created the nicest five-bedroom home on the block for a family of minks. If you do that, when you arrive back in the spring and turn the boat right side up, you will be greeted by a very angry mother of six mink pups. The eviction process is not pretty. Probably

best to store the oars on the outside of the boat for the winter, so you will have a means to defend yourself in the spring as you hold off that angry mink. Just a thought.

In cop speak, the subject boat was sitting in a lagoon, not too far from Bob and Carol's place in Ugashik. So, naturally, I would attempt to enlist Ugashik Bob's help to put the boat away. It's rare that I would make a solo trip down to Bob and Carol's Cabin. Each visitor at Camp Brewer waits with great anticipation for his or her chance to fly down to see Ugashik Bob and Carol. Bob and Carol have become rock stars in the minds of visitors at Camp Brewer.

Carol has achieved this status not because she lives in an isolated part of our world, but because she has relentlessly created a home, not just a shelter, in an unforgiving place. For as far as the eye can see, Carol's oasis is surrounded by tundra, which is vegetation composed of dwarf shrubs, wet grasses and, sometimes, swampy moss. Yet, Carol has mulched, tilled and loved her lawn to the point that it is the envy of visitors from stately manors. With flowers in full bloom, the average 'city-slicker' could get garden envy. There are no pine trees in the area, but Carol has 'poodled' alder bushes around the property to create the image of trees.

Carol and her home are just as beautiful on the inside. In Carol's heart, and home, there is always room for one more, without reservation or complaint. She is quick and easy with conversation and cares about what each of her guests have to say, whether you're eight or eighty-eight, a smelly fisherman or a retired Air Force General. There's hot coffee and fresh donuts for everyone.

The Campers who have not yet visited Ugashik, and met the legend of Bob, are probably expecting to meet a reclusive Great White Hunter type. To their surprise, upon their arrival in Ugashik, they find an intelligent, curious, engaging man. I think his fans have become enamored with Bob because he has effectively bridged two distinctly different worlds. As a retired IBM engineer, he is a computer guru, one of the people making the world spin. At the other end of the spectrum, Bob loves the out-

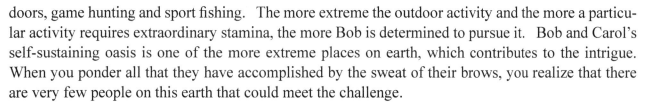

doors, game hunting and sport fishing. The more extreme the outdoor activity and the more a particular activity requires extraordinary stamina, the more Bob is determined to pursue it. Bob and Carol's self-sustaining oasis is one of the more extreme places on earth, which contributes to the intrigue. When you ponder all that they have accomplished by the sweat of their brows, you realize that there are very few people on this earth that could meet the challenge.

So, I asked Ugashik Bob if he would be willing to go with me to the Eggegik River to catch some silver, or coho, salmon. Bob asked me if I was going to use my fly rod or a "coffee grinder." He called people that used spinning rods coffee grinders. I love that. As we prepared for the trip, Bob smiled and said, "Must be time to put the boat away."

Actually, for this trip, I think Bob was anxious to get out of the house. I had a sense that Bob had something on his mind, he was carrying a burden. We arrived at the lagoon in the Eggegik River, and as we approached to land we spied fish sitting right next to the spot where the boat was parked. We would be parking the plane in a section of the river we call the "Lagoon." The Lagoon is an area of the river that is very wide, but shallow, not technically separated from the river, but has a barrier that would give you the impression you were in the calm water of a lake. Since the Lagoon is wide and shallow, the flow of the river in the Lagoon is extremely slow. The migrating salmon like to use the Lagoon as a resting-place, before swimming into the rapids of the river, which leads to their spawning grounds in Becharoff Lake. The Lagoon mostly consists of mixed-sand and small gravel, making it the ideal place to park the floatplane or a boat.

We parked the floatplane, nose first, on the shoreline. I hastily grabbed my fly rod. It was time to catch a few fish. There was no need to rig the boat to go fishing. I could simply stand in knee deep water next to the floatplane.

Bob did not take out his fly rod. Instead, he sat on the bank of the lagoon. As I quietly flipped a fly to the waiting salmon, Bob regaled me with stories from his life. Uncharacteristically, Bob began to talk about a number of things that were burdening him, nothing earth shattering, but we did discuss one problem that was more serious than the others. It opened the door for me to share my problems. Time together on the river has that effect, even when manly men are doing manly things.

With my limit of fish in hand, it was time to put the boat away. First, we turned the floatplane around so that the tail of the plane was hanging over the shoreline. Calm winds allowed this portion of the chore to be completed with relative ease. Since the bottom of the Lagoon is mostly sand,

we horsed the floatplane onto shore as far as humanly possible. We would be removing the outboard motor from the boat, carrying it to the plane for transport back to King Salmon. The closer we were able to get the plane to the boat, the shorter the distance we would have to carry the motor to the floatplane. We took the motor off the boat, tripped our way in knee deep water to the floatplane, laid the motor on the float and I climbed up on the float. Since I am smaller in stature than Bob, I crawled inside the fuselage of the plane while Bob attempted to pass the 125-pound motor through a small door in the back of the plane. Hey, if it were easy, everybody would do it.

We would next have to complete the chore of dragging the boat across the tundra. We usually have a way to cheat the system. The preceding year we brought four large pieces of six-inch pipe with us. We would lay the large pipe under the boat, so we could roll the boat up the bank on the pipes, instead of having to drag the boat across the tundra. Bob and I spent twenty minutes or so searching the surrounding area for our pipes. There were no pipes to be found, but we did happen to find a field of blueberries fit for a king. So we did what any respectable Alaskan would do. We found makeshift containers and filled them with wild blueberries. All berries in Alaska are edible, some only once.

We managed to burn a fair amount of daylight playing in the patch of blueberries. Enough with the diversion, it was time to get the boat stored. Bob and I then horsed the boat up the bank, Bob on the bow, me on the stern, with my back to the Lagoon. We got the boat to its winter resting place. Just as we were about to roll the boat over on its back, Bob said, calmly pointing to the Lagoon behind me, "Are we going to need that?"

When Bob pointed to the middle of the lagoon calmly gesturing, "are we going to need that" I was reading his facial expression. He didn't appear overly alarmed, so I took this to mean that perhaps a life preserver had fallen out of the plane and blown off shore. In that event, my neglect would cost me a $10 life preserver, as it floated away in the Lagoon.

I slowly turned around to see the floatplane had drifted off shore. It was now about thirty yards away, haplessly drifting in the middle of the Lagoon. Apparently, as we were looking for the pipes, okay, picking blueberries, the tide had risen. Although the plane was initially sitting high and dry on the bank, when the water came into the rising

Lagoon, it lifted the plane from the shore. Note to self: Always tie the floatplane to something on the shore.

No problem. We have a perfectly good rescue boat in our grasp. On the positive side, it's easier to drag the boat back down to the Lagoon. On the negative side, we had to drag the boat back up from the Lagoon. Oh well.

We completed the process. As we caught our collective breath, we sat down and continued our conversation. Bob revisited the burdens we had shared that day. At the end of our time together, Bob made a statement I will never forget. He said, "You put all of the problems of the world in a basket, drop your problems into the basket, then reach into the basket to grab a problem, you'd be happy to get your problems back." Bob knew how to put things into perspective.

I loved that day for two reasons. When Bob pointed to the middle of the Lagoon, calmly gesturing, "Are we going to need that?", it was the Mount Everest of sarcasm. Quietly hilarious.

More important to me were Bob's words to live by - about putting all the problems of the world in a basket including yours, then reaching in, and being happy to get yours back. Since that day, I have held onto that expression. Bob taught me a valuable lesson that day.

I WANT MY PROBLEMS BACK AND THE BACK STORY

Tim pondered his worries— as he meandered to Heaven's Bar
Wondered how his problems — Migrated so far

Heaven's was quiet — not a soul in the place
Save a bartender — with Rock Hudson's face
Wanting to drink — his troubles away,
Tim asked for "top shelf" — brandished his pay

The bar seemed mystical — with a scent in the air,
It smelled like fresh cookies — cotton candy, the fair
And the bartender — had that feel
Other worldly — it was truly surreal

Tim's frustration — witnessed his face,
Having big problems — such a disgrace.

He ordered another — prepared to confess,
His life is over — "it's really a mess"
He attempted to purchase — "a really trick car,"
Which ended with credit — as a complete bar
How would he explain — to his new bride to be
Such a big failure — no pride, you see

"In heaven's bar — there's a tradition,
If you don't follow — they say its sedition
Here is the basket — we split it in two
Fate will dictate — here's what you do."

"One side contains — problems of the world,
On the other you put in — money you've squirrel
Tim made his deposit — with dollar bills
Then he just stared at — the volumes of ills

"Now I can solve — your problems no tease
Reach in the basket — grab a problem with eas
Then you can trade — any problem with yours
You can relax — I'll keep the score"

As he reached in — Tim felt the jolt
A soldier's leg gone — like a lightning bolt
His leg had left him — as did his wife
He was struggling — to not take his life

Tim then reached in — to grab a new slip
His hand was still shaking — he lost his grip
This time he had taken — from a boy in Brazil
He was an orphan — his parents to pills.

Not liking options — he reached for a slip
This time he heard — the sound of a clip
A father had hidden — his only gun
But with neglect — he lost his son.

"I just can't take this — it's feelings I lack
I'd like to reach in — have my problems back.

"I need a few minutes — in the latrine
To comprehend — all that this means"

When he returned — a good look around
The good bartender — was not to be found
Then a new man — an angry face
"Sir, how'd you get — into this place"
"Where's the fella — spoke like a saint,
He said things — made me faint"

"I am the owner — it's just me,
I am here solo — only one key"
"Here's a contribution — for the basket of ills
Now that I get — the import of bills"
"Sir there's no basket — nor no face
I need to ask you — to leave this place"
As Tim walked — across Heaven's floor
Lots of white feathers — lead to the door.

© Ugashik Bob 2015

CHAPTER 4

Mr. Fox, Being with Empathy

IN WINTER, the Naknek River freezes, freezes hard. So much so that there are places on the river where the ice is so thick that motor vehicles use the river to cross from north to south, and back again. The water beneath the ice continues to flow. As the temperatures rise the ice breaks up, leaving huge bergs floating up and down the river. As the level of the water changes with the tide, the flow of the river changes directions, the ice in the river follows its course, and bergs of ice rise and fall with each morning and evening tide. A dock could never survive a winter or even a single ice-laden tide. Each year, in the spring, the ice disappears from the Naknek River, which is the sign from Mother Nature that it is time to open Camp Brewer. The annual ritual is to set up the screen porch, get out the fishing gear, put the dock in the water, get boats out of storage and the floatplane out of the hangar. Each of these tasks requires a crew of four or five skilled Campers. It's a lot of work. We say, "it takes a village." But unlike Hillary Clinton, not to raise a child or satisfy her husband, it takes a village to set up Camp. This particular year we were getting a late start. I am reminded that it was a late start because the Chinook make their annual migration up the Nushagak River around June 22. Now remember please, the village is called "King Salmon," so we will refer to the fish of the same name as "Chinook" salmon. King salmon, the fish, is also known as a Chinook salmon, one of five species of salmon found in Alaska. The other four are sockeye (also known as red salmon), the coho (also known as silver salmon), the pink (also known as the humpback salmon) and the chum (also known as the dog salmon). By the way, they call them dog salmon because you only feed those salmon to your dog or find them in buffet lines in small casinos located in obscure places.

Let's get back on track. One of the Campers was very anxious to get over to the Nushagak River, located some twenty-seven air miles as a raven flies from Camp Brewer. This is where Michael had his epic day the year before. We have a boat stored at the Nushagak River which also needed to be prepared for duty. By that I mean the boat has to be dragged down to the river, the motor tested and

run. We will call this Camper "Mr. Fox," because his goal on his visit to Alaska was to see foxes. Well, seeing foxes while catching a Chinook would require a true multi-tasker. Mr. Fox had volunteered for duty to get the boat going on the Nushagak. Although he was a newbie at Camp Brewer, one of the other Campers had tipped him off that there is an early run of Chinook on the Nushagak in or around June 22.

The life-cycle of a salmon is one of the most fascinating parts of nature, at least to me. Salmon release their eggs into the freshwater, such as the Nushagak River. A Chinook can lay up to 17,000 eggs. After laying the eggs, the spawning salmon attempts to cover the eggs in the gravel with her tail. Eggs that are laid, but don't get buried in the gravel by the spawning salmon, become immediately available as food for other fish, birds and insects. The female will stay in the spawning grounds to protect her eggs. If you have ever seen a picture of a salmon after it has spawned, you will notice that it grows gnarly cat-teeth, its jaws become elongated with the lower jaw becoming so hooked that only the tips of the jaw come together. The salmon's mouth, it's jaw line, takes on a shape that looks like an elongated football would fit in the opening. A native friend of mine told me that the shape of the mouth of a spawned-out salmon is the same shape of the tail of a salmon. After the female salmon has spawned, her mouth takes on that shape so that she can more easily use her mouth to grab the tail of a predator, pulling the other fish away from her eggs. She uses the shape of her mouth as a means to protect the eggs she has laid. It makes perfect sense. After spawning, Pacific salmon die.

One of the most amazing facts about Pacific salmon is their ability to return to their "natal" or home stream or lake. On the Nushagak River, this happens in abundance around June 22, each year. Salmon are thought to use several navigation aids to find their way back to where they were hatched. Scientists believe salmon use a combination of a magnetic orientation, celestial orientation, the memory of their home stream's unique smell, and a circadian calendar to return to their natal stream to spawn.

But I digress. Between the science, stories from the other Campers and folklore from the locals, Mr.

Fox was extremely anxious to get the dock in the water so that we had a place to put the float plane. He knew the floatplane would be our only means of getting to the Nushagak "to put the boat in the water." Wink-wink. Mr. Fox was carefully watching the tide come into the river, waiting for high water, or enough water to allow us to float the dock into place in front of Camp Brewer. Camp Brewer is nestled in the trees on the edge of the river, sitting next to a seventy-foot slope that leads down to the river. Naturally, we had to build a set of stairs that leads to the river. When the dock is out of the water, we need a place to store the gangway that leads to the dock. The stairs serve as a place to store the gangway or walkway for the winter. The gangway is on wheels. We simply roll the gangway up the stairs in the fall, to store it on the stairs for winter. In the spring, the process is reversed. The gangway is rolled off the staircase and down to the dock, which sits in the river. The gangway, then, serves as the bridge between the shoreline and the dock. Each time Mr. Fox suggested to the other Campers that it was time for a crew of Campers to help get the gangway off the stairs and the dock in place, he was the recipient of suspicious 'side-eye' from the other Campers.

It takes a crew of four Campers to get the gangway off the stairs, place the dock in the water and anchor the dock in the current of the river. No small feat. The crew includes a group of my friends willing to volunteer to help open Camp. These guys are the "MacGyvers" of the world, impersonators, really. If you saw these impersonators on the street, they would be holding a sign that says 'will work for fish.' Well, can you blame them? Most men will pretend to be capable of anything that gets them a chance to go salmon fishing. But the process of opening Camp requires we have a cast of characters including a person impersonating a boat mechanic, a MacGyver plumber, a wanna-be construction specialist, and a real aviation maintenance professional. The first three can pretend to be anything. The aircraft mechanic has to be the real thing. If the pretend boat mechanic neglects to do his job, the motor of a boat quits. Consequently, one finds oneself floating down a river. When the motor of an airplane quits, one finds oneself screaming as the little houses in the distance below start to get bigger and bigger. So, we need a real aircraft mechanic in Camp.

We had planned to get up early in the morning, set the dock pieces into the river, and roll the gangway onto the dock. With great anticipation, Mr. Fox about had a nervous breakdown when he woke up that morning to find the tide extremely low. The area in which we intended to locate the dock was high and dry, sitting thirty yards from anything that resembled water. There would be no placing the dock in the water this particular morning. Eventually, we did get the dock and gangway in place. Mr.

Fox and I checked our survival gear, gathered a small amount of fishing gear, climbed in the floatplane, and made an uneventful trip to the Nushagak in clear blue skies.

The boat that is located at the Nushagak River is stored outdoors all winter. This isn't exactly the Hamptons. There isn't the option of storing your boat inside a building. When we arrived at the Nushagak, we found the boat intact but full of water. The gent - I'll call him Mr. Crown because he drinks it by the barrel - who was responsible for looking after the boat had removed the plug from the boat, just like a plug from a bath tub, but the high winds during winter had blown leaves into the boat, clogging the exit drain. It rained excessively in the spring.

In the spring, it is Mr. Crown's expectation that you will pay for winter storage upon your arrival. Actual dollar bills are nice, but Mr. Crown also accepts, you guessed right, Crown Royal, in lieu of dead presidents as payment for boat storage. I feared that another patron had submitted a recent payment, which may be the reason my boat looks like a bathtub. We located a couple of empty plastic bleach bottles in Mr. Crown's trash pile, cut the bottoms off the bottles, and went about scooping the water out of the bottom of the boat. We could see Chinook salmon rolling in the river. Occasionally, a fisherman would hoot and holler. Nothing gets a guy scooping water out of the bottom of a boat like the sound of fisherman yelling "look at the size of that one." Yes, Mr. Fox was a very motivated scooper. The louder the fisherman, the more intense the scooping. When we finally got all the water out of the boat, we attempted to get the motor going. Naturally, the motor wouldn't start. This is an annual event for me - broke shit! To be expected. But, Mr. Fox had just arrived from the big city. His temperament was still in city mode. I was on river time, taking things in stride. It took an hour or so, but we got the motor running.

A slightly less intoxicated Mr. Crown showed up just in time to collect his payment, drag the boat down to the Nushagak River, and remind us to "be a friend and spend." When he saw that we had removed two empty bleach bottles from his trash pile he said, "That'll be extra." This is the prime season for Mr. Crown, so no opportunity to make money is ignored. Mr. Crown, effectively has three weeks to make money. When the fish are gone, so are the tourists, so Portage Creek becomes a ghost town. He also runs a temporary General Store, which is a shipping container that teeters on the edge of the river. He gave us the thrill of watching the Alaskan version of a used car TV commercial – live from Alaska: "We're open for business - so, be a guy and buy!" Something to behold. I don't mean to poke fun at Mr. Crown, he is actually one of my favorite characters in the Alaskan bush. I do so look forward to seeing the ever-unpredictable Mr. Crown each year.

I asked Mr. Crown if he would hold the bow of the boat while I attempted to get the motor started, to which he replied, "That'll be extra." As Mr. Crown pushed the bow of the boat off the shore into the river, Mr. Fox witnessed the glory of the Nushagak, as three boats sitting downriver from our launching point were all hooked up on Chinook. To Mr. Fox's bewilderment, we pointed the boat up river. Mr. Fox

looked at me in dismay. We were moving away from an area that obviously contained massive numbers of fish. "Why are we leaving fish, to go up river to find fish?" I responded, because if the motor quits, and they do, I want to be able to float in the current of the river back down to the plane. If we start fishing down river, the motor quits, and it will, we will have to drag the boat three miles against the current up the river." We drove the boat several hundred yards up river, cut the engine, drifting with the flow of the current back towards our home base and Juliet Yankee.

Mr. Fox promptly hooked into and landed a beautiful Chinook. It took ten minutes to net and unhook the fish. With the lengthy distraction of tending to the fish, neither of us had seen a wall of fog approaching from the east-side of the river. Camp Brewer sits twenty-seven miles to the east of the Nushagak. The fog was creating a wall, a barrier, to our ability to fly home. I told Mr. Fox to quickly store the fishing gear, we needed to depart immediately if we intended to sleep in the comforts of our own beds tonight.

We hastily put the fishing gear away, but slowly prepared the plane for flight. Fortunately, the Nushagak River, at least in the area we were parked, flows north to south. We took off to the north, with a plan to fly low and slow over the Nushagak, parallel to the fog bank. If or when the bank of fog dissipated, we would turn to the east and head home to Camp Brewer. We continued to fly north, but apparently Mother Nature did not agree with our flight plan. We flew for twenty minutes, no joy.

When we left Nushagak, we had two hours of fuel on board. The fog was forcing an extended diversion to the north, away from Camp Brewer, which sat to our east. We flew an additional ten minutes.

We had burned about 25% of our fuel supply in that half-hour. The wall of fog persisted. We knew that it was clear where we came from. The door was still open behind us. The wall of fog was a constant, consistently remaining on the east side of the river. We could turn around, follow the river for the entirety of our trip back to the Nushagak, with an hour of fuel in reserve for the morning flight to Camp Brewer. We did just that. We safely landed on the Nushagak, back at Portage Creek.

We hiked up to Mr. Crown's cabin, lugging the single most important item of emergency gear for our survival in Portage Creek, a 750 ML bottle of Crown Royal. This is what Mr. Crown calls a day bottle. Seeing a pattern? I asked Mr. Crown if he had a place for us to stay. He said that all his tents and cabins were full, but there was an old trappers cabin off the beaten path that would serve as shelter for the night. Mr. Crown, now in his soiled longjohns, pointed to a bear trail six-hundred yards to the southwest of the spot we had parked our boat. "Follow that trail, and that'll be extra." There we would find "Trapper Jack's" cabin. It was now getting close to midnight. Fortunately, it was just after the summer solstice, so we could make the hike in complete daylight. As we approached the cabin it became apparent that Trapper Jack had left the cabin, and earth, at least a generation ago. The last visitors, who were from a law firm we will call "Brown and Harry," had pushed the door off its hinges. As we climbed over the door, we found two 'beds' in the cabin, each mysteriously resembling picnic tables sitting side-by-side.

Mr. Fox was quick to call dibs on the picnic table next to the window. The wind had picked up, making it difficult to get the door back in place. It was after midnight before we were able to get the door secured. Mr. Fox laid down on his picnic table with his head next to what he thought was 'the window.' As the wind kicked up, the window started to move. But not in the way a typical window will rattle in the wind. The window started flapping, like a flag in the wind. Mr. Fox realized that the window was actually a piece of clear plastic sheeting. Mr. Fox astutely asked, "Was that really a bear trail that we used to get to the cabin?" I assured him that very few humans have a need or reason to use that particular trail, certainly not Trapper Jack's maintenance crew. Mr. Fox quickly repositioned himself so that his feet were next to the window. I giggled. Mr. Fox asked, "What?" I laughed a little louder and opined, "Life is full of difficult decisions. Apparently, you have decided to lose your feet and not your head."

"Goodnight, John Boy", I said.

"Goodnight, Mary Ellen", he replied.

We returned to Camp Brewer to a fanfare fit for Super Bowl Champions. Mr. Fox was more than satisfied, arriving with a Chinook and the story of a lifetime.

Unfortunately, I came home to sad news. Although there was a crew of four useful Campers, there was one very dispensable Camper. Number five. we will call him "Mr. Sympathy". Mr. Sympathy was a client of my law firm. He hails from somewhere east of the Mississippi and he was not my favorite person in the world. By extending an invitation to a client, I had made the mistake of attempting to mix business with pleasure, something I would live to regret. Mr. Sympathy lacked a soul. He was not a religious man. Not that religious affiliation assures one of having a soul or of being a soulful person. But, it was clear that his family would visit church three times in their lives - "to hatch, match and dispatch." That which Mr. Sympathy lacked in faith-based training was not made up by natural spirituality. Two things motivated him: food and money, in excess and in that order. Yes, I had sold my soul.

Mr. Sympathy advised me that while Mr. Fox and I were delayed on the Nushagak, a person by the name of "Peter" called. Anyway, Mr. Sympathy reported, "I thought the dude said Peter, but he had a heavy French accent.' This 'Peter' had left an urgent message for me to call home. He said my friend Tim had an accident.

Tim and I had spent two years working together on an airplane project. When I left California, we were close to completing the project. I say "we." Tim had hired a Frenchman, Pierre, to assist him with the project. Pierre was a student of aviation at the local community college. Tim and I

were close to getting the airplane flying. Over that time, I had spent untold hours with Tim. When you work in and around an airplane together for extended periods of time, you had better get used to working closely with another man, figuratively and literally. These are tight quarters. Like working in a submarine, but smaller. In sum, Tim and I had become quite close in that period of time.

Over the course of our time together, I would learn that Tim was the second child to two wonderful parents. He had three sisters who loved him dearly. Since Tim grew up with three girls, he loved, respected and knew how to treat women. As we worked together on the airplane, Tim talked about the times that his sisters invaded his space and snooped in is room, but Tim put up with them. He loved his sisters. Tim would describe to me that he enjoyed his time in the basement of his home in Ohio, building model airplanes, spending time with his schoolboy friends. As a young man, Tim was the 'audio visual guy' in high school. He was the guy with the funky, big glasses. He was a geeky kid with a grin that was a combination of Jim Carrey and Timothy Olyphant.

Tim's family didn't have a lot of money but what they did have was the classic midwestern work ethic and tenacity. At the age of thirty-three, Tim's father lost his eyesight. While his father was in and out of hospitals his four children were split between relatives, living in separate homes in Ohio. This went on for a period of over four years. Unfortunately, Tim and his oldest sister drew the short straws. They ended up living with an aunt and a mean-spirited uncle, enduring the unspeakable. Especially Tim who was just five years old at the time. Some people are just evil.

After recovering from surgery, his father received an opportunity to move to Lima, Ohio, to sell Kirby vacuum cleaners, which became a family affair. From home showings to cold calls to appointments, Tim and his three sisters each took turns driving their Dad on appointments to sell vacuums. Tim's father was so good at demonstrating and selling the Kirby vacuum cleaners that many of his customers did not believe he was blind. He would become a motivational speaker for the Scott and Fetzer Co., the company that built the Kirby vacuum cleaners.

Tim's father did not let his blindness interfere with his love for aviation. When Tim was young, his father bought a 1947 Stinson Tail Dragger. His father would hire pilots to fly him around his hometown. This is where Tim got his desire to make aviation the focal point of his life. Tim was the product of great people. As a friend of mine aptly described him, Tim was an "artist and an engineer." We all thought he was a genius. I certainly did.

Before I left California for my annual trip to Alaska, Tim and I discussed the possibility that we would convert Juliet Yankee from a floatplane to a ski plane. We hatched a plan to put skies on Juliet Yankee in the coming winter. After converting Juliet Yankee to a ski plane, we would take a ten-day, 1100-mile trip following the Iditarod dog sled teams from Anchorage to Nome.

As I sat at the kitchen table with Mr. Sympathy, I attempted to make sense of Mr. Sympathy's handwritten message. When I looked at the telephone number I realized 'Peter' was actually 'Pierre.'

When I called Pierre, he reported to me that Tim asked him to go grab some burgers at the local hamburger joint. Upon Pierre's return, he crossed paths with an ambulance exiting the airport. When he returned to the hangar, Pierre learned from a fellow pilot, who happened on the scene, that Tim had passed out. He was found unresponsive on the floor of the hangar. This had happened several days before Pierre's call. Pierre reported that Tim had melanoma. The cancer had found its way to Tim's brain.

Pierre said that I needed to "prepare for the worst." As Pierre reported this to me on the telephone, Mr. Sympathy was sitting next to me at the kitchen table. I was visibly shaken. Like I said, I had become very close with Tim and his family. Hearts would break. Tim was in his mid-50's, brilliant, with a wonderful life ahead of him. He had a very full head of naturally brown hair, and was healthy, happy and excited about life. It was his dream to build the plane. We were having fun together, like boys in a basement.

When I hung up the phone, Mr. Sympathy asked what had happened. Through my shock, I did my best to relate the entire story to him, providing him with the details of our history together. I explained to him that Tim had cancer. I ended by telling Mr. Sympathy that the prognosis was not

good. Mr. Sympathy asked, "What kind of cancer?" I replied, "Melanoma." Mr. Sympathy exclaimed, "Oh my God, how do I NOT get melanoma?" My face began to boil. Not slowly. Catching himself, he said, "Oh, you'll have to send Tim a card."

I would never forgive Mr. Sympathy. I would never forget his reaction to what I reported to him, to what he witnessed. For many years, I have held on to the anger that I have felt for Mr. Sympathy. Over that period of time the bitterness has risen in my heart.

To me, Mr. Sympathy was ugly from the outside in and the inside out. I have been angry with him for a long time. My advice to my 59-year-old self was, "Anger is poison to your body. If you hold on to the anger that you feel for someone else, it is like drinking the poison and waiting for the other person to die. Mr. Sympathy isn't drinking the poison, you are."

What I really wanted for Mr. Sympathy was for him to feel empathy for Tim, for his family. Over a lifetime, I have realized that empathy is such a deep emotion - it cannot be taught. While the expression of sympathy is a kind gesture, which has a time and place in all relationships, it is a very different emotion than empathy. Tim succumbed to cancer before we made our trip to Nome. But, he did get to fly in the plane he built.

Any time I experience a stirring of emotions a poem is sure to follow. Perhaps the rhythm of a poem creates a sense of calm in me, despite the fact that my mind insists on expressing feelings that are intense.

JUST BEING WITH EMPATHY

The other day — I took a walk with Empathy
As we walked, I asked Empathy — about her brother, Sympathy
"You know Sympathy, — it's all about him
We shouldn't waste our time on Sympathy — how's your brother Tim?"

"Tim is declining — the Cancer is here — yes, it's worse- worse than we feared"
As Empathy spoke next — her words cradled Tim
"I'm sure he'll walk with God — I love him"
When Empathy expresses herself — it's as if she lives in Tim
Empathy is beautiful — from the outside- in

Up walked Sympathy — with no grace to display
— feeling the pain of others — is not his way
"I heard about Tim — it's Cancer he's caught
It's an affliction I worry about — quite a lot"
Sympathy stood there — surrounded by lard
"Oh, I'll have to send — Tim a card"
Sympathy can be — driven by guilt
When others suffer — Sympathy just wilts
Sympathy is not — Empathy's match
Sympathy thinks Cancer — is something you catch

Understanding Sympathy — is all for naught
Expression of emotions — just can't be taught
Empathy said "Sympathy — from your point of view
— Nothing bad ever happens, — until it happens to you"

To be with Empathy — is a beautiful thing
To be with Empathy— makes my heart sing

In Loving Memory Of David Scott Rado
December 1, 1952 to December 9, 2004

CHAPTER 5

Mr. Eagle, The Grass Is Greener

LATER THAT SUMMER, we entertained a rather large group of Campers. I was downstairs before day-break, enjoying the quiet of the morning snuggling with a warm cup of coffee. A mid-forties Camper stumbled down the stairs. He would join me to enjoy the tranquility of the river. As we drank coffee and watched the river we conversed. It is tradition for me to ask each guest, "What is your mission here in Alaska, and what would you like to see or do?" He said that he wanted to catch a grayling using a fly rod and see a bald eagle, so I will call him "Mr. Eagle." Mr. Eagle wanted to know what it was like to spend summers alone in Alaska. I regaled him with stories of fishing, flying, and wildlife viewing. He wanted more, but I didn't really understand what he was looking for. He was probing, really. I had a sense that there was a certain need to know "What was a lawyer from California doing in Alaska, alone?"

He was dying of curiosity. He just had to know the "real" reason I was in Alaska. There are so many stereotypes in life, but Alaskans have their own stereotype. I am certain you know all the stereotypical statements that are used outside of Alaska. I don't really think it is necessary for me to revisit them here. In fact, it would be somewhat disheartening for me to outline them for you in the year 2018. Perhaps a generation ago an author could justify providing a laundry list of examples of stereotypes to help you understand his meaning, but no good purpose would be served here and now. But there is an Alaskan characterization worthy of mentioning and you may not know this one: "Everyone that comes to Alaska is running from something." I suppose in an odd way I had become a victim of profiling. Mr. Eagle was a very nice fellow, but as our polite conversation progressed he eventually lost his patience and finally blurted out the real question. "When did you get divorced, or are you still married?" The unspoken message: 'You must be in Alaska because you are running from something, perhaps your marriage.' I replied, "Still married." To add to his confusion I added, "I think the Mor-

mon way is correct – the greatest gift a father can give his children is to love their mother." When I quoted the Mormon philosophy, poor Mr. Eagle was about to lay an egg. I think he believed there would be no alcohol served at dinner. But, I actually do believe the Mormon philosophy with respect to family values. Except to my way of thinking, it's not about "family values" – it's about "valuing family." I had not lost sight of the fact that Mr. Eagle was a guest in my home. I wanted him to feel welcome. So, we would spend the next hour or so getting to know one another.

You see, Mr. Eagle was more of a friend of a friend. Mr. Eagle had ridden the coattails of our mutual friend to arrive at Camp Brewer. I'm not complaining, just explaining. There is room for that kind of loyalty in some relationships. Prior to the trip, my friend relayed to me that Mr. Eagle was a stockbroker from New York. I observed that he was a very fit, athletic, overall attractive man. Not gorgeous. When telling me about Mr. Eagle, and his family life, our mutual friend had explained that Mr. Eagle had two young daughters. I will call them Emma and Eva because it has a certain cadence to it as you read or say it. Emma and Eva. Emma was a freshman in high school and Eva was in her first year of middle school. Emma and Eva were both straight 'A' students. Emma was a star athlete. Eva was the head cheerleader.

Mr. Eagle's wife, we will call her 'Farrah' (I know, I had the poster too), was an attractive forty-year old x-ray technician. Mr. Eagle, in his sober state, was responsible, well grounded. His wife, Farrah, was more ethereal. She had her head in the clouds. Farrah had a certain wanderlust. Left to her own devices, she would have lived in a trailer and flown first-class to Paris. It was her goal to start her own travel agency. This would satisfy her free-spirited dream to see the world. She had a gypsy's soul.

I never learned if Emma and Eva were close to their mother. Like a lawyer, I only heard one side of the story. I did learn that Emma and Eva had expressed a desire to go to college, including postgraduate school, and had pre-selected their colleges of choice. It is hard to imagine, given that they were in middle school and the early years of high school, that both girls had already decided on their choice of colleges. Impressive. About three cups of coffee into the morning I suggested that a group of us fly down to Featherly Creek.

We flew to Featherly Creek and made the trek across the tundra chatting and getting to know one another. Mr. Eagle checked his first box, catching a series of grayling with relative ease. Mr. Eagle would join me next to my 50 caliber semi-automatic, as I did my best to stand guard while the other two Campers caught fish. After sitting together for a bit, Mr. Eagle finally formed his version of that all too familiar phrase, "A man in your profession must hear a lot of divorce stories. I know you don't know me that well, but do you mind if I ask you for some personal advice?"

As we sat on the edge of the creek, Mr. Eagle went on to explain that he and Farrah had drifted apart. He was interested in active sports, while Farrah preferred watching movies. He wanted to purchase a new bike, Farrah new clothes. He wanted to go to the Masters Golf Tournament, Farrah wanted to see Rome.

As we talked, I did my best to remind Mr. Eagle that at some point in time, he and Farrah had something in common, at least in their college days. Yes, admittedly, during their college years they both enjoyed riding bikes to the park and reading together. He would read Surfing magazine. She would study art and literature. They would walk hand-in-hand to a dinner destination on the edge of the park where he would share his thoughts about adventure, she about literature, and both about their future together.

Mr. Eagle and I sat, talked and watched the other Campers catch fish. One ambitious Camper had thrown caution to the wind, placing two flies on one line. He had a dry fly located about thirty-six inches from the end of his fly line. The dry fly would float on the surface of the stream, having the appearance of a mosquito that landed on the surface. On the end of the fly line he had fastened a simulated leech, which has long black feathers and looks like a leech swimming in the water, which sank to the bottom of the creek. Suddenly, the floating fly disappeared as the water opened up into the mouth of a grayling. At the same time, the other end of the line headed the opposite direction from the grayling. A char had swallowed the leech. The Camper had caught two fish in a single cast. Unheard of.

Both fish were now flailing on the surface of the water. As they splashed, the Camper did his best to release the char without injury. At the same time, the grayling continued to splash on the surface of the creek. All that noise from the splashing made me uneasy. It was like ringing a dinner bell for a bear. My mind raced as I recalled the number of significant bear events we have had during our visits to Featherly Creek. According to the scorecard that I was keeping, we were up to four major bear events. I was not excited about the prospects of a "Yahtzee."

I will briefly tell you about three of the events, lest you be filled with ennui. But first, you have to understand the geography surrounding Featherly Creek. The hike from Becharoff Lake to the edge of the creek crosses mostly flat terrain. As you approach the creek, there are places a hiker can simply enter the creek on level ground. There are no fish in that area of the creek. But if you hike further up the creek, where all the fish are located, the creek sits deeper in a ravine. A fear of heights would not get the best of you - you're not standing on the edge of the Grand Canyon. At the highest or deepest point of the ravine, depending on your perspective, the ravine is only thirty feet deep. In this area, you have two choices. Your first choice is to approach the area adjacent to the creek, taking a path through thickets of alder trees. Not a problem, if you enjoy being in close quarters with brown bears. A more conservative approach, for people who want to live a long life, would be to approach the creek in the area of the terrain that is open and flat, at the top of the ravine, overlooking the creek. This approach has two advantages. First, a Camper can walk directly to the creek with an unobstructed view to ensure the brown hairy things are not around. Second, when you arrive at the creek from this vantage point, on flat ground and on the top of the ravine, you are peering down into the water with a great view of all those fish.

One day UB2 and I took the ravine approach. We safely made the hike from Becharoff Lake to the edge of Featherly Creek without getting eaten, save by a few hundred mosquitoes. As we approached an unobstructed bend in the creek we were at the top of a ravine looking down at a pool of grayling and char. Awesome. But now the challenge was to get down the sandy bank of the ravine without disturbing the fish. Decidedly not possible. We conceded the issue, sliding down the thirty feet on our bottoms. As we did so, the sand predictably slid into the creek, and the fish promptly scattered. No bother. We simply hiked up the creek knowing the fish would regroup there in the next couple of hours. We would save this spot for the final casts of the day.

After a day of fun, more for us than the fish, we returned to the bend in the creek adjacent to the thirty-foot wall of sand. We were deep in the ravine. Two large swaths in the sand, representing the imprints from our collective buttocks, marked the path up the ravine toward the safety of the floatplane. UB2 and I stood with our backs to the sandy bank, mindlessly making casts across the twenty-five feet of water that separated us from the bank on the other side of the creek. UB2 is a great fly caster. I'm not so great. But even beginners can cast the width of Featherly Creek. The quiet of the moment was lost when UB2 exclaimed in an agitated voice, "BEAR." UB2 and I had reached an understanding years before. If we were ever dangerously close to a bear, one of us would simply yell "BEAR" to let his companion know we had a bear on top of us. It was a drill we had discussed for years. This was no drill. I looked up to see a head the size of the backboard on a basketball hoop protruding from the alders. We immediately started our chant "HI BEAR, HI BEAR, WE ARE MOVING BEAR." But, where? The sandy wall of the ravine behind us served as a barrier. If we attempted to vacate, we would both be crawling on all fours up the sandy wall of the ravine. I have watched enough episodes of Mutual of Omaha's Wild Kingdom to understand that most things that get eaten by bears in Alaska walk on four legs. This was not a good time to impersonate bear food by scurrying up the ravine on all fours. Worse yet, and yes, it can get worse, the bear was upwind from us. He couldn't smell us.

With the ravine as a barrier to our exit, and the creek in front of us, our only choice was to walk back up the creek in the direction of the bear. As we started to walk up the creek towards the bear our heads were lowered so that the bear wouldn't interpret our behavior as an act of aggression. Specifically, heads down, no eye contact. The bear, in turn, started to slowly walk down the opposite side of the creek. There was now twenty feet of deep water between us. UB2 whispered, "He is headed to the shallow part of the creek so he can make the crossing." UB2 and I were both walking with pistols in hand, hammers cocked. This was not a drill, people! We made it about ten or so yards up the creek. The bear was now downstream from us as we were about to initiate our disappearing act deep into the alders on the opposite side of the creek. The bear began to cross the creek, now in ankle deep water. I was very glad I was wearing my brown pants today. This was it. Just then, I felt a light breeze sweep across my back, as if the feathers of an angel tickled my neck. Relief, wind at my back. The wind whisked across the back of my neck and head, peacefully flowing to the nose of a certain bear. When the scent of this stinky Camper struck his nose, Featherly Creek exploded as the bear darted into the alders, taking with him a swath of trees as wide as a single lane highway. It sounded like a tractor being driven through a forest.

I stood there, hand shaking. I looked at UB2. I looked at the cocked pistol in my trembling hand. I held my thumb on the cocked hammer, slowly squeezed the trigger to release the hammer to a safe position. UB2 said with a grimace, "We really need to take up bingo."

The next two bear incidents can be described in Reader's Digest format. One day, Harry and I spent an afternoon together fishing Featherly Creek. Harry is one of the magnets that keeps me heading towards magnetic north. Harry went up the creek, I went down. As I fished my way up the creek, I turned a bend to witness Harry running full steam down the center of the creek, attempting to cross in knee deep water. I yelled at Harry, "I thought we don't run!" he replied, "We do when there's three of them." Loping behind Harry was a massive bear sow with two cubs. Best to give her space.

The next event involved Mr. Sympathy. I calmly arrived at Featherly Creek with the oversized Mr. Sympathy. We saw bear after bear. Our group was continuously being pushed down the creek. I cautioned Mr. Sympathy that, although we don't run, we needed to move quickly. Mr. Sympathy, trying to catch his breath, explained that he was carrying the equivalent of a two hundred-pound man on his back. The bears continued to push us. This discussion repeated itself three times through three bends in the creek. The bears sensed we had a weak link. They continued the assault, pushing us slowly downstream. I implored Mr. Sympathy to hasten the pace. He was doing his best. Ultimately, I conceded the issue, substituting my normal chant "Hey Bear, Hey Bear" for "Hey, don't crowd boys, there's enough for everybody." I finally attempted to lighten his load by setting Mr. Sympathy's lunch and fly rod off to the side of the creek. I guess that a certain fox sensed my frustration with Mr. Sympathy. Seriously, though, it would be the last time I would take any person who is not physically fit, or at least capable of carrying their own weight, to Featherly Creek.

Back to current events. I am understandably on guard while the lucky Camper releases his two fish. Mr. Eagle continues with his explanation, expressing great pride in the fact that his daughters were doing extremely well in school. He expressed that, even to that day he found Farrah attractive, intellectually and physically. Mr. Eagle indicated that he and Farrah were in agreement that after the events of September 11, the entire family should move from New York to the West Coast. As Mr. Eagle talked I was thinking, "his life with Farrah doesn't sound so bad."

And then, thud. Mr. Eagle dropped the infidelity bomb on me. Mr. Eagle said that he was currently involved in an extra-marital relationship with a research analyst at work. People have affairs. No

judgment here. As Mr. Eagle and I talked, a couple of birds, magpies, landed on the shore of the creek, picking up scraps of salmon left by marauding bears. So, I will call the other woman "Maggie". He described Maggie as athletic, telling me that she enjoyed active sports and liked to party.

Keeping my best priest face, I processed the information Mr. Eagle was providing me. I couldn't figure out, in the short time we had together, what had motivated him to have an affair. And why he had selected me, two steps removed from being a stranger, as the person to whom he confessed the affair? Perhaps he just needed to unload the burden of his infidelity, or he assumed some apparent attorney/client relationship bound me. Maybe he viewed the relationship as priest/penitent and he presumed I would sit on the other side of the confessional curtain, simply nodding my head without passing the story onto God. In actuality I did wish that we were sitting in a confessional booth, separated by the anonymity that a curtain provides. But there we were, face to face.

I asked Mr. Eagle, "What would make you happy for your lifetime? What is important to you in the big picture?" He said that he wanted to love, and to be loved. He wanted passion, to feel 'that spark' in his relationship. He also wanted to be a family and enjoy family events. He wanted to see his daughters grow up, go to college and have happy marriages and families. He wanted financial freedom, time to do things in the outdoors. He wanted his partner to be supportive of his desire to live an active lifestyle.

As he spoke I had a flashback to a story I heard while attending a church service with a friend of mine during my years in college. I may be out of my depth in my attempt to recall the story, but here goes. As the story went, the captain of a ship had traveled from Europe to the Atlantic Ocean, close to Florida. The captain and a large crew of men entered the Gulf Stream in the Atlantic Ocean. The Captain had miscalculated his speed and direction. Worse, the ship had a limited supply of fresh water. Despite his years of navigation by dead reckoning he became further disoriented. He became lost in the ocean's currents. Too much time and distance had passed for him to make it to shore to get fresh water, and so he had imperiled his crew. The captain made the decision to ration water, but it was too late. As he approached the edge of panic, with very little water left in the hull, the crew spied another ship. A crewman signaled the other ship, informing them, "We are in distress, please bring us water." It was at this point that they received a signal from the other ship, "Lower your buckets, you are in the Gulf Stream. There is fresh water all around you." Despite the fact that the ship was in the open ocean, presumably in salt water, fresh drinkable water was actually in abundance in the Gulf Stream. The Gulf Stream current is a remarkable fresh water river within an ocean as it crosses the Atlantic Ocean connecting Florida and southwest Great Britain. The fresh water that the crew needed was all around them.

Mr. Eagle was in the Gulf Stream in his marriage to Farrah. Mr. Eagle had expressed to me that he thirsted for love, passion and family. It was like the fresh water in the Gulf Stream. He didn't know it but salvation was all around him. He simply had to lower his bucket. Instead, he was about to leave fresh water to find salt water. To my way of thinking, he was about to needlessly die of thirst.

Then he used the old saying, "I guess the grass is greener on the other side of the fence." I replied, "Yes, but in the coming years you will learn that you have to mow and fertilize on that side of the fence too." Seven years from now, when Maggie gets that proverbial itch, he will find that he and Maggie will have a multitude of issues that need to be negotiated. The 'grass may be green on the other side,' but he is going to have to mow and fertilize on Maggie's side of the fence as well. She will change with time. He will change with time. People do.

I explained that if he left Farrah he would create an abyss of uncertainty. Had Mr. Eagle considered the possibility that Farrah, who by all accounts was an attractive woman, would meet a new man? Since his daughters were in middle school and high school, this new man would become a part of their lives for at least the next few years; that this new man would become an integral and integrated part of the lives of his two daughters. If Mr. Eagle were not present in the day-to-day affairs of his daughters he would not be as available to provide input with respect to who his daughters were dating, for instance. Had he considered that holidays now had a different look and feel? He and Maggie may want to have a Christmas celebration. Farrah and her new partner would also want to have their own celebration. His daughters would get married and their in-laws will want to have a holiday celebration. With the division of the family his daughters would now have four families to make happy instead of two. Since his daughters may feel duty to make everyone happy, there was the potential that no one would be happy.

As we hiked from Featherly Creek back to the floatplane parked on Becharoff Lake, I sensed that Mr. Eagle was burdened by our conversation. The discussion had created a tumultuous state in my mind. With the turmoil came a poem:

THE GRASS AIN'T GREENER

These midlife stories — I bite my tongue
It's a struggle — to NOT be young
The answer is not — a new mate
Sure—the novelty — can be great

The grass is green — on the other side
But over there — mistakes don't hide
On that side — grass needs mowed,
Fertilizer-water — seeds be sowed

In kids minds — families are forever
Mom and Dad — are their tether
All those pictures — in their minds
Stay with them — for all time

A misconception — "they're all grown"
"They'll recover — hearts be sewn"
Truth be known — words are choked
Pictures remained — hearts are broke

Hearts remain — by the family fence
As you age — it all makes sense
If there's grass — that must be mowed
Journey complete — with your kids in tow.

© Ugashik Bob 2015

CHAPTER 6

Master Bird, Wild Fish

I MUST WARN YOU IN ADVANCE that at the end of this chapter, there is a poem that is intended for children. The material is not graphic and may not be suitable for adults. I continue…

One of my favorite guests under the age of ten (save one, of course, but he was not a guest) at Camp Brewer was a nine-year-old boy I will call Master Bird. Master Bird came to Camp Brewer with his father, Racer. He was, and remains, one of my favorite guests because as Racer, Master Bird and I were driving down the driveway away from Camp Brewer heading to the airport in King Salmon, Master Bird summed up how I feel about Alaska in one sentence. Master Bird inhaled as if he were about to swim the length of an Olympic swimming pool and as he exhaled the exasperated nine-year-old exclaimed, "Dad, the best day of my life is when I came to Alaska, and the worst day of my life is when I had to leave." A brilliant little philosopher that effortlessly communicated an emotion in a single sentence that I could not convey in an entire book.

During my time with Master Bird we managed to shoot with bows and arrows, ride ATV's, shoot guns, fly floatplanes, play horseshoes, canoe down King Salmon Creek, view bears, foxes and eagles, and of course, catch salmon. During a fishing trip with Master Bird to the Eggegik River we managed to catch our limit of wild, coho salmon in a matter of minutes. There were so many salmon swimming in front of us that I was able to rig my flyline with a large, pink floating fly that mimicked a mouse. As I tugged the pink mouse across the surface of the calm, clear waters of the Eggegik River, salmon after salmon would rise to the surface in an effort to take down the pink mouse. It was laughable, and we laughed.

I asked Master Bird if he was excited to eat fresh, wild Alaskan salmon for dinner. He inquired, "Is there any other kind of salmon? Isn't all salmon the same?" I asked, "What kind of salmon does your Mom buy at the market?" Master Bird replied, "She buys the Atlantic salmon." I thought, "Aha, a teaching moment!" I then went into my diatribe about the difference between Atlantic salmon (Atlan-

tic, Scottish), which is typically farmed salmon, and wild Alaskan salmon.

Master Bird was not convinced. He said, "It all tastes the same to me." In a last-ditch effort to make a difference in the life of young Master Bird, I said, "It may taste the same, but farmed salmon will not nourish and strengthen your body into a healthy man. Farmed salmon won't put hair on your chest the same way that wild salmon will." Master Bird said, "I'm not sure I want hair on my chest."

I didn't want to let it go. I gently explained that, "When you go to the market with your Mom to buy fish you will see some labeled 'farm-raised' and some labeled 'wild' or 'wild-caught.' Sure, they're both salmon, but they're very different things. A farm-raised fish was raised in some kind of aquatic farming operation, not in the wild. Salmon farms are different sizes and from different parts of the world. Farmed salmon will differ in the same way that a carrot farmed in Mexico differs from a carrot farmed in California. The farmed salmon are raised in net-pens or closed tanks which are completely cut off from open ocean. Wild salmon, as you'd probably expect, are caught in the wild. Many of our friends here in King Salmon take their boats, usually at the mouth of the Naknek or in the Kvichack Bay and head out to catch these fish in their natural habitat. This means when you eat a wild salmon you are not only eating healthier food, you're supporting our friends in the villages which surround us."

The diatribe continued, poor Master Bird. "Wild salmon eat plankton which make their meat a rich red-orange color. The plankton is a luxury that fish farmers cannot afford. Instead, farmed salmon eat pellets containing synthetics and their meat is dyed red to mimic the look of a wild salmon. Without the dye, the meat of a farmed salmon would be a gray tone. A happier, healthier free-roaming salmon will deliver a more 'salmony' flavor and color. The colors of that wild salmon we caught today will be more vibrant than that of the farm-raised stuff, more red-orange than pink. The flavor will be much more tasty. Wild salmon have less fat than farm-raised salmon." Master Bird's reply, shrugging, was, "Okay." So, I guess I was now officially "off the clock."

This is not the first time I have lost a debate surrounding wild versus farmed salmon. I once en-

tered a quiet bar in Costa Mesa, California. I was there for lunch, and there was only one other patron at the bar. The remainder of the guests of the restaurant were sitting on the patio. I ordered a glass of red wine because the only time anyone should have white wine is when the restaurant is out of red wine. As I looked over the menu, I was craving wild salmon, hoping the restaurant would serve only wild salmon, but if they served farmed I would have the chicken instead. The bartender was a spunky 25-year-old woman. Her tattoos communicated that she wished to be perceived as edgy, which she was.

I have made it my habit and objective to educate people down in America (I know) about the perils of eating farmed salmon. I take every opportunity I can to inform anyone who will listen about the benefits of eating wild salmon. I take the position that farmed salmon is poison. To that end, I asked the bartender, "Is the salmon you serve wild salmon?" She said, "No, sorry, it's farmed." I replied, "Oh, I am so glad you know the difference. In that case, I will have the chicken." In a loud and sarcastic tone she brilliantly replied, "WHY? Because THAT'S not FARMED?!" Wow. Dial 911. That hurt! Only because she was right. What's the difference between farmed chicken and farmed salmon? Point well taken. And, yes, she got the full 4%, gratuity. No need to be petty.

So, back to my fishing trip to Eggegik with young Master Bird. It is understandable that a young boy should not be concerned about the difference between farmed salmon and wild salmon. After all, most of America has no hesitation about hunting down their next meal in a drive-thru, fast-food restaurant. The issue of whether they are eating wild versus farmed salmon is the least of their worries.

That night, I feared that I had done a poor job of explaining the health benefits of wild salmon to young Master Bird. We can't expect children to be concerned with the complexity of the debate over farmed versus wild salmon. This is an issue for consideration by thoughtful adults. Heck, most adults don't even appreciate the difference. I thought it would be a better use of my energy to sit down and explain this concept in a simple way for the benefit of children, and other living things. So I've tried to create a simple explanation in the poem that follows.

SARAH THE SALMON

Sarah the salmon — swam by my net
My friend Frank said — "I'll take a bet
Even with — all the world's charm
That beautiful Salmon won't love — a fish from a farm"

Getting her attention — was my biggest wish
Using my best line I yelled — "are you tickle- fish"
"Too bad I'm a fish — you can't see I'm laugh-crying"
"By the way, farmed fish — are only for frying"

I longed to be a native — fresh from the deep sea
Not sure that she would ever— love a farm boy like me
For me it was love — love at first sight
In full living color — her skin was so bright
I was from a fish farm — so just black and white
Living behind a net — it was my plight

Sarah had muscles — as she leaped with joy
So Strong and gorgeous — a real 'fish- Tom -boy'
It's hard to grow strong — where it's dark and it's dank
When your life exists — in a fish tank.

Thousands of us live — behind this fish net
It's been a year — since we first met
Soon Sarah will — head out to the sea
I just pray — she won't forget about me
She won't compute — her boyfriend is farmed
And while she's at sea — that she won't get harmed

It's now been three years — I sit, thumbs twirled
While Sarah looks for health food — all over the world
They give us antibiotics — and pellets of soy
Clearly not the best way — to make a man from a boy

I wish you could tell me — all you've endured.
It will be four years — before we exchange words
It's then that I'll tell you — about my friend Frank
He died suddenly — something infected our tank

During the autopsy — his flesh was still gray
The red dye neglected — to create a fillet
The man from the autopsy — he just joked
He said Frank's "skin — it looks like he smoked"
Four years have passed — how do whales sound?

Maybe you'll tell me — as you are home bound

Your brother just swam by — his flashy skin
I asked about you — he just flipped me the fin

Your brother, he circled — said I'm "not your guy"
I said, "I can look different — they'll add the red dye"
"I know that we both have — a similar taste
But you spent your whole life — in the fish waste
It's not just that — you need minerals from the sea
Sarah is wild — a real fish you see."

Words of wisdom — her brother he said.
Words us farmed fish — have come to dread

"In a world that struggles — to define true wealth
We define it — with good food and good health
So even as our lives — come to an end
We all hope — that we remain friends."

"Like her ancestors — as a new day dawns
Sarah will swim up stream — in good health to spawn"

CHAPTER 7

Mr. Wolf, Nature's Choice

WHEN MY SON, Chap, and I first went to Alaska, he was nine years old. I took him down to the mouth of the Ugashik Lakes where I knew we would find an abundance of salmon. Chap was very excited to wear waders for the first time, stand in the water up to his waist and drag salmon back to the beach. Naturally, he did not want to wear a life jacket. You might say that I tricked him by making him wear a vest that contained an auto-inflate life jacket. The life jacket has the appearance of a normal fishing vest. But the vest that he was wearing that day had a self-contained life jacket, with an automatic air cartridge. Should young Chapman inadvertently end up in the water, a paper wafer attached to the air-cartridge would get wet and expand, which would cause the air cartridge to be activated. As a result, the life vest would automatically inflate. These are great for small children and pets, but they are not recommended for mothers-in-law. You should never let her wear one.

As Chap ventured into the waters of the Ugashik River, he would cast his fishing line, reel the line in and take another step into deeper water, closer to the rapids of the river. I admonished, "Chap, be careful, it gets deep fast and the river will take you away like a kite in the wind." Chap said, "I know Dad, I know." Another cast and another step. "Chapman, that's far enough." Chap: "I know Dad, I know." Yet another cast and still further he goes. "Son, that's far enough -" Chap, "I – WHOA!," and off he goes. It was his good fortune that the auto-inflate feature worked perfectly. I scrambled down the bank of the river paralleling my son as he bobbed like an apple in the rapids of the river. As the rapids turned towards the shoreline, I grabbed him by the scruff of the neck and yanked him onto shore.

Chap: "Am I in trouble, Dad?" He had already received the equivalent of a paper cut from Mother Nature. There was no need for me to pour lemon juice on it. I said "Chap, I think you have already learned a valuable lesson. Now let's make a fire so we can dry out these clothes."

It was at that point I realized that it would be essential for me to pick and choose the trips into the bush for Master Chapman or anyone else under the age of twelve years old. Which meant that I would

have to find myself a suitable babysitter.

That night Chap and I headed for Eddie's Fireplace Inn for a couple of Belly Busters. A Belly Buster consists of two charbroiled beef patties, two strips of bacon, two slices of melted American cheese, mayonnaise, ketchup, pickles, lettuce and tangy French Dressing, all on a seeded bun. It was among Chap's favorite things to do in Alaska.

As we sat down in the dining area at Eddie's, an attractive young woman came from behind the bar and approached our table. Eddie's is a bar/restaurant. A half-wall separates the bar from the dining area. The young woman was doing double-duty that night, acting as a bartender while serving food in the dining room. She had a heavy Australian accent. To say that she had an air of confidence would be an understatement. "What'll it be, fellas?" Her demeanor could best be described and depicted as mirroring Berta on the sitcom "Two and a Half Men." She was an Alaskan version of Berta in spirit, but not in her physical appearance. So, I will call her Berta. Chap placed his order, a Belly Buster, no mystery there. Berta first brought Chap a small salad, which Chap completely ignored. When Berta returned to the table she said with a smirk on her face, "Eat your salad or you'll find it in your bed tonight." Chap laughed.

After dinner I asked Berta if the internet at Eddie's was working. She replied, "Sure. Me and the boys have been watching porn all afternoon." Clearly, Berta was capable of handling a room full of boys. I was thinking I had found my babysitter. I cautiously explained to Berta that Chap and I would be spending the summer in King Salmon. On occasion, it would be nice if I could have some alone time in the outdoors, in areas that would not be safe for a young boy. I asked Berta if she would be willing to watch Chap, and friends, from time to time. She agreed.

By and by our relationship with Berta evolved. Eventually, my brothers would ask if I would be willing to entertain customers from their company. Their biggest customer at the time was Oakley, one of the world's largest manufacturers of eyewear. My brothers invited two executives from Oakley to

Alaska, to Camp Brewer. As luck would have it, both of the executives were experienced fishermen, so it would be easy to provide entertainment. I was a little nervous because Oakley represented millions of dollars in revenue to my brothers. I needed to ensure that everything went perfectly. I would need assistance with household duties. I asked Berta if she would be willing to help with the cooking and cleaning. She reluctantly agreed.

Berta organized a menu, purchased the food and came to Camp Brewer early in the day, before the honored guests arrived. Having spent time with Berta in the past, it was my practice to give her the space she needed to do her job. She enjoyed listening to music, cooking and being left alone. She is a deep thinker. I stayed comfortably outside her safety zone. I hoped that she would enjoy her time at Camp Brewer. I believe she did.

The two guests, the "Oakley Boys," had arrived. One of the two Oakley Boys was more aggressive than the other. He came on like a lead balloon. I will call him "Rusty." Rusty was a very fit, 40+ year old man of Japanese descent. He sat down at the kitchen table, uncomfortably inside the safety zone that Berta had created for herself while preparing dinner. Envision an area around a helicopter pad, within the area in which the main rotor blades of the helicopter are spinning. Better that you not get inside that safety zone, lest you lose your head. As Rusty began to interrogate Berta, the hair on the back of my neck stood up. I prayed Rusty wouldn't engage Berta. I was certainly capable of providing entertainment while fishing and flying. But playing referee between Rusty and Berta? "Standby one."

Rusty started the small talk. "So, Berta, where you from, England?" Berta replied, "No, Australia." Rusty then launched a missile over the bow of Berta. "Yeah, England, Australia - it's all the same." And now from Berta, "Rusty, where are you from, China?" Eyebrows raised. Rusty replied, "No, Japan." In lightning-fast response, Berta replied, "Yeah… Japan, China, it's all the same."

Oh, flag on the play! I had to intervene. "Careful Rusty. The man that upsets the Camp cook, BECOMES the Camp cook."

Berta demonstrated that she was capable of holding her own with any man. Her next challenge was a house full of boys. The next group of Campers included four fathers and six boys ranging in age from middle school to freshman in college. One evening, as Berta was making dinner, a group of five boys and two Dads were sitting around the kitchen table. The Dads were enjoying cocktails. Berta was minding her own business, in her safety zone. Had Rusty left her alone the week before he probably would not have gone to bed with a bloody nose. Anyway, one of the boys exclaimed, "Berta, I am going to skip dinner, my stomach hurts." Berta, again within a nano-second, "Let's solve this here and now. You either have to poop or you're having girl troubles. Which is it?" Oh, my!

Later, as dinner was served, it was like a scene from a prison movie. A group of inmates at Camp Brewer were scrambling for food as Berta placed a stack of burgers on the table. One of the boys, pushed his mate yelling, "Watch it, you fag." Berta was quick to intervene, "Hey! Gay men deserve your respect because they look each other in the eye."

I locked eyes with one of the Dads who was standing by the table. He was visibly affected by Berta's comment. The issue was yet to be defined. Was it the gay slur, or was there more to be concerned about? I perhaps needed to prominently display a sign in the kitchen that read: "The Opinions Expressed Here Are Not Necessarily Those of the Management." Berta's joke was not the spirit of Camp Brewer. Berta was extremely offensive at times, but she was kidding as she often does. Everyone is fair game at Camp Brewer, lawyers included.

This particular Camper, the concerned father, had come to Camp Brewer with the goal of seeing a wolf. So, I will call him Mr. Wolf. It was at that point that I knew Mr. Wolf had a real concern. Mr. Wolf had a look of shock on his face. I didn't get the impression that the gay remark had offended him. I had the impression, feeling really, that Mr. Wolf was reacting with a certain paternal instinct. It was as if he was thinking that his son was in real danger. If I could compare the scene to a movie it was as if Mr. Wolf was watching as his inattentive son left the safety of a crosswalk, entering a busy city street, and wandering into traffic. When Berta made the fag comment, Mr. Wolf wanted to grab his son and pull him out of harm's way, back into the safety of the crosswalk.

As I have previously mentioned, I have a gay brother and two gay nephews. I have been witness to many such uncomfortable moments throughout my life. I was no stranger to the body language that accompanies a parent struggling with his child's sexuality. Nor was I unfamiliar with the struggles of the child.

That night I was sitting alone with Mr. Wolf on the screen porch, sipping red wine. I asked him, "What is your mission here in Alaska. What would you like to see?" He replied, "I would love to see a wolf. Also, I have heard a lot of good things about a place called Grovesnor Lake. Do you know it? I understand they have some good trout fishing over there." I told Mr. Wolf that going to Grovesnor would be no problem. It is just a fifteen-minute ride in the floatplane to Grovesnor. But seeing a wolf would be a rare event.

I then relayed a story about our only wolf sighting. There was a summer at Brooks Lodge when a wolf joined four bears at Brooks Falls. It is a fascinating event to watch the bears at Brooks Falls. Each year the brown bears gather at Brooks Camp because it is one of the first streams in the area to receive an abundant supply of fresh salmon. In July, most salmon are moving through large rivers and lakes. It is difficult for bears to successfully fish in large bodies of water. It is much easier for bears to catch salmon in slow water, where the salmon are in a confined area. Another prime spot for bears to catch salmon is shallow water where the bear can pounce on the salmon, trapping the fish with its front paws. Early in the salmon run Brooks Falls creates a dam, a barrier for the fish. Brown bears accumulate in the pool of slow water below the waterfall where they gorge on salmon. There have been times when we have stood on the platforms with eleven bears in our field of view. Immediately in front of us, above and below the waterfall, four bears will compete for fish.

To provide perspective on this event, imagine that each of the four 'Brooks bears' is a high school student, a freshman, sophomore, junior and senior, respectively. The largest of the bears, a senior, obviously gets the best fishing spot at the falls at Brooks Camp. During the heaviest run of salmon, the largest of the bears might stand in the prime spot at Brooks Falls catching a salmon every eleven minutes or so. The high school junior will get the next best fishing spot below Brooks Falls. That spot might yield a salmon every twenty minutes or so. The sophomore, a less desirable spot, yielding a fish every half-hour, and so on. Now, imagine that a very large college football player appears on the scene. A senior lineman from Ohio State. He will slowly lumber over to the smaller high school senior, give him a look, as if to say, "move out of my spot, squirt." As the more dominant bear begins to slowly circle the high school senior, the two bears exchange shallow growls. As a matter of pride, the high school senior lowers his head, avoids eye contact with the college football player, very slowly circles while acceding to the request of the more superior bear. The high school senior gives up the

prime fishing spot. The high school senior then saunters over to the junior and repeats the dance. Eventually, the freshman finds himself patiently waiting on the sidelines for the carcass of a dead salmon, the equivalent of a wayward doggy bag, to float by.

There was a year when four such dominant bears were doing their dance. The largest of the bears was sitting in the prime fishing spot, catching an average of five fish an hour. The other four bears were doing their best. Along came a wolf. This is no fairy tale, no red riding hood here. The wolf sat on the fringe of the Brooks River, in ankle deep water. He waited, watched and pounced, grabbing a salmon his first try. Ironically, the bears ignored him like he was a schoolboy, a nuisance. The wolf continued to fish with the bears. In the hour that we watched the wolf, he caught seventeen fish, while the best of the fishing-bears caught only six fish.

It is something we have not seen, before nor since.

The following day, I took Mr. Wolf, among others, on a short trip to Grovesnor Lake. Grovesnor is more than a place to fish, it is a place of beauty and seclusion. But there is fishing - as a matter of fact, great fishing for rainbows, char, lake trout, pike and sockeye salmon. Camp Grovesnor sits on the narrows of a river between Grovesnor Lake and Lake Coleville. Yes, Grovesnor and Coleville have their own version of 'the narrows.' These narrows also have excellent fishing. Camp Grovesnor backs up to the Aleutian Range, surrounded by glaciers. As you stand in the waters of the narrows, the lake, the Aleutian Range and monstrous glaciers are all in a single point of view, serving as a surreal backdrop. There are two rivers accessible from Grosvenor Lake which are the largest spawning streams for sockeye salmon in the Naknek area, getting over 100,000 fish each annually. One of our favorite things to do at Grovesnor is wade out into the water to within a few inches of the top of our chest waders. Basically, one more step would result in extremely cold water pouring over the top of our waders. Invariably, we get wet. Why? Because it's worth it. There we will stand, shivering, to wait for birds to begin dive-bombing the water. The birds come screaming in from all angles, like warplanes attacking an unsuspecting harbor full of boats.

As we fish, the dive-bombers have spotted a school of lake and rainbow trout surface-feeding. If you've never seen this phenomenon, it looks like the lake's surface is boiling, and it happens when schools of lake and rainbow trout force schools of smaller fish to the surface. While the fish are surface-feeding, the birds are attacking the small fish as they are forced to the surface by the trout attacking from below. It is at that instance that we feverishly attempt to cast our flies, which simulate the small fish, to the center of the boil.

It doesn't happen all the time, but it happened that day for Mr. Wolf.

We would spend the day together at Grovesnor Lake. Mr. Wolf seemed to have reached a certain level of confidence in me. Mr. Wolf was a religious man. We talked about his men's bible study. The guest that invited Mr. Wolf was someone that I respected. He, too, was staunchly Christian. My friend, or the guest that I was closest to, had conveyed to me that he had great respect for Mr. Wolf's intelligence, patience and love for God.

Eventually, I would apologize to Mr. Wolf for Berta's fag comment during dinner. I didn't say this to Mr. Wolf, but it was fairly obvious that his son is gay. He had a flamboyant wardrobe. As a fisherman, he would definitely be a glittering excess (I know). There were other signs, too. Needless to say, as a brother and uncle of three gay family members, I cheerfully lend support to parents and children as they are "coming out." I love my brother, Christopher. I only wish he had come out sooner.

I was curious about how Mr. Wolf would handle this dimension of his life. Had Mr. Wolf reconciled this issue with himself and his faith? Is homosexuality something that lands on the side of God? Is it no big deal?

As the fishing winded down, it seemed to me that Mr. Wolf was still agitated. He wanted to get something off his chest. As Mr. Wolf and I sat alone, breathing in the wide-open space, eating a sandwich, he told me that his son (I will call him "Master Wolf") had come out to him - that his son was gay. He went on to tell me that he was concerned about Master Wolf. Mr. Wolf was conflicted, and I am summarizing here, Mr. Wolf could not accept his son's homosexuality. And, to his way of thinking, neither would God. He was not sure that Master Wolf would make the list in terms of getting into heaven. I think Mr. Wolf misinterpreted the look of surprise on my face. He most likely thought that I was troubled at the revelation about his son. Au contraire. Rather, I was somewhat shocked that Mr. Wolf believed his son would not make it onto God's list.

Mr. Wolf went on to tell me that he held out hope that Master Wolf would get married, in the traditional way. His belief was based on the fact that in high school he hung out with the most beautiful

young women, therefore he clearly had an interest in women. Despite the revelation by Master Wolf, Mr. Wolf was still hoping that Master Wolf would make a different choice. In my mind, God had created Master Wolf to be a gay man. There was nothing on God's green earth that would change that fact. Gay was not, and is not, a choice.

I paid a bit more attention to Master Wolf after Berta made the insensitive comment. In his time at Camp Brewer, it seemed to me that Master Wolf was withdrawn, not really engaged like the other boys. Given what I had just learned, it's no wonder. At this point in time I was a tourist, an observer. My only contribution was to listen and perhaps share my family's experience.

To me, it was as natural for Master Wolf to be gay as it is for the earth to rotate counter-clockwise or for rain to fall from the sky. If Mr. Wolf were to ask Master Wolf to make a different choice, to pretend to be heterosexual, he might as well ask the world to spin backwards. Mr. Wolf wanted his son to defy gravity, defy nature.

Before I went to bed that night, I thought about Master Wolf. He had come out. I was happy for him. Master Wolf could stop holding his breath now. But as for his father, I went to bed with a heavy heart. I must have been dreaming because I woke up mid-sentence, with a voice yelling at me, yelling, "Make the world spin backwards - slow down that hurricane!" There are times when I have had a dream, only to roll back over and fall back to sleep. As I rolled over, I had every intention of remembering the dream so that I could tell the 'weirdest dream' story the following morning. Usually, when I wake up, I have no recollection of the dream. On the other hand, some dreams feel so real I feel like I'm watching myself on the big screen at the theatre. During dreams like that don't you so wish you could crawl into the screen to help yourself? You ask your mind, "Why in the hell am I not helping myself? Do something!?!" Those dreams can leave you shaking for hours. This was more like a big screen dream. I was not going to roll over, fall back to sleep, and forget the yelling. I had great empathy for Master Wolf. I laid awake for a while, thinking that Master Wolf must fear that he had no voice in the matter. He was being censored, muted. So with these thoughts, I wrote this poem:

NATURES CHOICE AND BACK STORY

It's not easy — to be gay
There's so much — I have to say
Why do you want — to take my voice
Why do you say — "you have a choice"

(yelling): — "MAKE THE EARTH ROTATE
BACKWARDS"
Are you afraid — God will judge me
Why don't we just — wait and see

(yelling): — "SLOW DOWN THAT HURRI-
CANE"
I have a lifetime — to love you
I hope you — will love me too

(yelling): "MAKE THE RAIN FALL FROM THE
GROUND"
No word of a lie — I tried to be — "be that guy"

(yelling): "STOP BEING LEFT HANDED"
Some things — are God's to say
It's nature — that created Gay
You see — I have a voice
Being Gay — was God's choice

Crisis averted? Not really. The following day we went to Brooks Falls. When we returned home, Berta had dinner on the table. A crowd of Campers surrounded the dinner table. In a repeat performance from the night before, one of the middle school boys called someone a fag. Berta sarcastically interjected, "He's not gay, he was just there first." Mr. Wolf and I, again, locked eyes. The wound was still fresh. Can his son endure a lifetime of inept jokes? Can Mr. Wolf? When we talked about it the day before I felt like we took a full step forward. Now Berta unwittingly sent us back ten yards. I hoped our dear Berta had not created the tipping point, the point at which Mr. Wolf would unknowingly begin to sabotage his son's efforts to come out.

Mr. Wolf and I retired to the screen porch to drink a glass of red wine. We delved into it again. At the end of the evening I said to Mr. Wolf, "Before we turn in for the night tonight, can I share one last thought with you?" "Of, course," he replied without hesitation. I took a deep breath. "There is no safer place in the world for a child than his own home, agreed?" He nodded in agreement. "In his home a child is surrounded by family, perhaps brothers, sisters, aunts, uncles, etc., he or she is free to take risks, to be himself, to experiment, to embarrass himself, all without judgement and with the unconditional love of his family. This is the child's safest place in the universe. We both know that once we leave the safety of our home, the world can be a cruel place. Right?" Again, he nodded in agreement. "It's imperative that a child be given the earliest possible opportunity, if he is gay, to reveal that fact, all within in the safety of his own home. His home is one of the few places in the world he will feel acceptance, unconditional love and the freedom to discover how to have a relationship both he and his family can be proud of. One of my biggest regrets in life is that I didn't know that my younger brother was gay until I was thirty years old. If I had known sooner, I think I could have been a better brother. I could have been a source of greater support, as a brother should."

We sat on the screen porch, fire blazing, and talked about it until the wee hours of the morning. I went to bed wondering if Mr. Wolf would "let it go." By 2AM I decided to take energy to pen:

ADAM AND ADAM AND EVE

Who killed the story of Adam and Adam?

— Did they do it on a lark
Were there two boys — on the Ark

Like a bluff that slips away — did some-
one — erode the gay
What if heaven — does not hex?
Perhaps in heaven — there is no sex.

Two Adams or an Eve — God has some-
thing — up his sleeve
As they rise — through heaven's mist
I'm sure all three — make the list

Chapter 8

What About Bob?

I DON'T KNOW WHAT IT IS ABOUT ME, maybe it's a major character flaw, but I have a sense of urgency to race through that proverbial bucket list. The urgency to live life to its fullest smolders like a fire burning inside me, each and every day. When Tim died it was like throwing gas on that fire. It has been eleven years since Tim took his walk with God. In our hangar, I still have the white board with our handwritten note – our plan to fly the Iditarod together. I can't bring myself to erase our note. As Ugashik Bob says, "We're burning daylight." As a result, I was more determined than ever to complete the trip to Nome in a ski plane. One night, I was having dinner with a group of friends. One thing, as in drink, led to another. I started talking about my intent to fly a ski plane. "We will follow the dogsleds along the Iditarod Trail to Nome." My friend Bob Brown or 'Bobby" as his friends know him said, "Life is short, I am in."

Bobby loved Alaska. He had come to Camp Brewer the previous summer for a four-day trip. He ended up staying eleven days. He called it his "epiphany trip." Let's be honest here. Alaska is like heroin, only Alaska is more addicting. Naturally, Bobby's trip to Camp Brewer included an excursion to Ugashik to see Ugashik Bob and Carol. When Ugashik Bob met Bobby, he asked Bobby, "What do you do for a living?" Bobby explained that he was the 'Vice President of Sales of Infusion Disposables for an internationally known manufacturer of medical devices.' Ugashik Bob responded, "So, you're a professional 'Sunshine Pumper.'" Bobby loved it.

But Bobby is not just a sunshine pumper, he's the ultimate sunshine pumper. Bobby is one of the most gregarious, sometimes hilarious, personalities I have ever met. He has the extraordinary ability to make friends and acquaintances wherever he goes. When Bobby is in the room he is creating energy all around him. If you ever meet anyone engaged in the business of selling medical devices, they know Bobby. The best way to describe Bobby would be to say that people like Bobby sit at the center of our social universe, bringing all of us together. He is the hub. Bobby has the ability to connect with

people and connect people. When he is around, all the activity revolves around the energy he creates, socially and professionally. But then, as Ugashik Bob said, Bobby is "a sunshine pumper."

Earlier that year I had convinced Bobby to become my partner in a helicopter. The only problem with my proposal was that neither one of us had a license to fly a helicopter. I know at this point you must be thinking I need a 'check-up from the neck up.' At the time Bobby and I purchased the helicopter, the Robinson Helicopter Company had a six to eight month wait time from the date of purchase of the helicopter to the date of delivery of a new helicopter. When we put down our deposit on a helicopter, I immediately started flight school. Admittedly, I had a head start in the process since I had a fixed-wing pilot's license. I received my helicopter pilot's rating thirty days later. I continued to fly with my helicopter flight instructor, James, for the succeeding six months. Naturally, it was our goal to fly the helicopter to, where else but Alaska?

Bobby took helicopter flight lessons, intermittently, for the following six months. Bobby tells an amusing story about trying to hover a helicopter during flight training. Bobby was sitting in the right seat (in a helicopter, the pilot in command sits in the right seat, opposite of the scenario of a fixed wing). His female instructor was sitting in the left seat. Bobby described his helicopter flying thusly: "I was trying to hover and the helicopter was swinging violently in all directions. It was like watching a monkey trying to have sex with a football. I yelled in frustration, 'What am I doing?!' The instructor grabbed the controls away from me and said, 'I have no idea!'" That would be the end of his lessons with that particular flight instructor. Since Bobby was not happy with his flight instructor, I suggested that he gain some flight experience by flying our helicopter home from Alaska with my flight instructor, James.

The following fall, Bobby and James did just that. After I returned to California, I was at lunch with James, Bobby and a group of friends. I asked, "How was the flight home with Bobby?" James replied, "First, don't call him Bobby. He wants to be called 'Chopper Bob.'" Bobby confirmed the declaration, without interrupting, with a huge smile. James continued, "As you know, we left King

Salmon early one morning, heading for Homer, Alaska. Bobby insisted that he occupy the right seat, typically the seat the pilot occupies. Despite his confident stride towards the commander's seat, Bobby had a total flight experience of zero point zero hours. I started the helicopter as Bobby struggled with fitting his headset properly over his traditional aviator sunglasses. A few moments later, I lifted the helicopter skyward and we were airborne towards our first stop, Homer. As we flew over the southern shoreline of Iliamna Lake, I hopefully handed Bobby the controls of the helicopter. Suffice it to say, controlled flight was brief, as the helicopter attempted to return to earth in a somewhat inverted manner, despite Bobby's best efforts. I dutifully assisted Bobby, coaching him through the basics of straight and level flight. We refueled the helicopter in Homer as quickly as possible, and the hopscotch continued down the coastline of Alaska."

As James was relaying the story, there was no opposition from Bobby, now 'Chopper Bob,' so James continued, "With pure grit and a high degree of determination, Chopper Bob managed longer and longer periods of time in which the helicopter remained generally upright and pointed in the direction he intended. In those harrowing moments, 'Chopper Bob' was born. The weather turned typically Alaskan, deteriorating rapidly so I flew the helicopter at lower and lower altitudes, in less and less visibility. We touched down in Ketchikan having not flown much above 200' for that leg of the trip. I called for a fuel truck. The young refueler asked Chopper Bob, 'What kind of fuel would you like, captain?' Bob looked at me in despair, so I quickly rescued Chopper Bobby with, 'One-hundred low lead.' Chopper Bob picked up the conversation with the refueler from there. 'Yup, we had to make a few turns back there and had to use more collective pitch than planned, but thankfully Chopper Bob had things under control.' Chopper Bob, casually referring to himself in the third person, explained the harrowing last few minutes of the flight to an unsuspecting refueler. 'Wow, that sounds crazy!' the refueler said. 'Yup, Chopper Bob always has things under control.' The intrigued refueler then asked, 'How many years have you been flying?' With the utmost swagger, Chopper Bob responded, 'Oh, well it's

been...' Chopper Bob glanced at his watch, 'Oh... about eight hours now.' The refueler looked at Chopper Bob and chuckled. He looked over at me and asked, 'Is he for real?' I looked at Chopper Bob and in a respectful tone I said, 'There's no one better than Chopper Bob, don't let him fool you.' The refueler rolled his eyes, looked up at the thickening clouds, and said, 'Good luck, Chopper Bob. You're going to need it.'"

Bobby truly is a Sunshine Pumper, and one hell of a salesman.

So, we have let 'stories of Bobby take us off on a rabbit trail.' Bobby will do that to you. Be careful. We need to get back to the dinner down in America. I told Bobby and friends that I intended to complete the trip to Nome in late February and early March of the following year. But there were three obstacles. First, the preceding fall, my plane Juliet Yankee was destroyed in a hangar fire in Naknek. So, we did not yet have a ski plane. Second, we did not have skis for a plane. The final obstacle was that I had never flown a ski plane. Bobby said, "Dude, life is short, so I am in." I responded, "Bobby, no joking, you have to commit now, because I will buy a plane that is capable of flying on skis, I will find skis for the plane and, I will hire a pilot to teach me to fly the damned thing." In his most reassuring voice, Bobby said, "Tic-Toc, Tic-Toc, the clock is ticking, I am in." I wasn't entirely sure that I believed him. I loved the guy. I wanted to believe him. But there was only room in the plane for me, two passengers, and survival gear. He would be on the short list of people that I would be willing to take on the trip. My first choice was Harry, who lived in Alaska, and was a dog-musher and knew how to survive in the winter.

In lawyer speak, soon thereafter (sounds like where lawyers go when they die), I purchased a plane in Willow, Alaska, that would serve our purposes quite well. Her tail number is Zero Four Tango. She had a very large engine, no interior and was about as ugly as a plane could be. The perfect ski plane.

I found a pair of skis that would fit Zero Four Tango. One minor problem. The skis lived in Ely, Minnesota. Zero Four Tango lived in Willow, Alaska. I bought the skis, shipped them to Alaska, and then hired an aviation mechanic to install the skis on the plane.

In the early part of the winter, I traveled to Alaska to meet with the mechanic, check on the progress of Zero Four Tango and purchase supplies for the Iditarod. I still had my doubts about Bobby's level of commitment. So… standby for the evil Bobby scheme. In anticipation of the upcoming Iditarod trip, I borrowed a pair of snowshoes from my mechanic. I walked over to a frozen lake and hailed down a local ski plane pilot. I asked him to take a well-staged, picture of me standing in front of his ski plane, which created the appearance that I was dressed for the Iditarod. When I returned back to America, I had the picture made into a post card. You can call it a premonition, but I had a sixth sense that Bobby was going to stand me up for our date in Nome.

I spent the next several months gathering survival gear, reading every possible book available on the subject of flying a ski plane on the Iditarod trail, and otherwise. I attempted to include Bobby in the discussion and preparation. We were both excited. To be fair minded, I knew I was half-crazy to buy a plane, put it on skis and fly to Nome. If I myself knew I was insane, Bobby had to be sharing in the despair. Despite our shared enthusiasm, I seriously questioned whether Bobby was crazy enough to make the trip.

In February 2007, I boarded the flight from Los Angeles to 'Los Anchorage.' I had, in hand, survival gear, aviation maps from Anchorage to Nome and a blank post card containing a picture of me standing in front of the ski plane that I had taken some months before. Actually, the post card was pre-stamped and pre-addressed to Bobby. I just didn't know what to write. The plan, at that point, was for me to spend a day or so flying the ski plane with an instructor. Thereafter, Harry and I would spend a

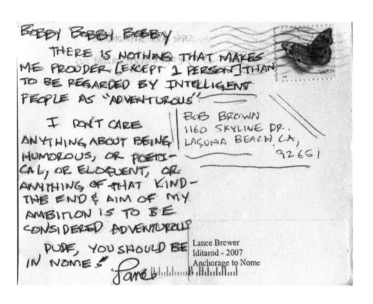

few days flying up the Iditarod trail to Un-alakleet, where I would confirm that Bobby had made it on his commercial flight to Nome. Once I knew that Bobby was heading to Nome, I would go to Nome, pick up Bobby and rejoin the Iditarod teams in Un-alakleet. But would Bobby actually show up in Nome?

All I needed was the courage to call his bluff. If I were to call Bobby's bluff, and send the postcard in advance of his departure date, what should I write?

I filled out the balance of the post card as follows:

"Bobby,
There is nothing that makes me prouder than to be regarded by intelligent people as "adventurous." I don't care anything about being humorous, or poetic or eloquent, or anything of that kind. The end and aim of my ambition is to be considered adventurous. Dude, you should be in Nome!
        -Lance"

When I arrived in Anchorage, I stood in the post office for about ten minutes procrastinating, as if I were in Las Vegas staring at a spinning roulette wheel, dumbfounded. Is Bobby really going to show up in Nome? If I mailed the postcard now, and Bobby did show up in Nome, he would call me a jackass because I didn't believe he would show up. But if I mailed the postcard and he didn't show up in Nome, he's still going to call me a jackass!! As I watched the roulette wheel continue to spin, I heard the final call, "Place your bets!" I mailed the post card. That night, having bet the farm against Bobby, I wrote a simple poem that seemed appropriate at the time.

TIC - TOC

Life it passes, so very fast — I wish certain moments, would ever-last
Tic Toc, Tic Toc — can't anyone, hear that clock

Where is the urgency — To live life?
Not in most people — there is strife

They procrastinate — think and wait
Then they realize — it's too late

CHAPTER 9

The Iditarod

NOT VERY MANY PEOPLE KNOW, but the Iditarod is actually a tribute to Alaska's history, a recreation of an event that took place in 1925. That year, twenty different dog teams carried diphtheria serum six-hundred seventy-four miles over a rugged trail from Nenana, Alaska to Nome, Alaska. The trip took one-hundred twenty-seven-and-a-half hours and it saved the village of Nome.

The annual race - The Last Great Race - started in 1967 to commemorate the 1925 event. Harry and I were on a once in a lifetime trip, flying a ski plane from Anchorage to Nome. I wanted to capture the spirit of the event for the benefit of my young son, so I kept a handwritten journal of the events that took place each day.

The following are excerpts from the journal.

Chap: 3/3/07: I started this trip with a preconceived notion that Alaska is a wild, unforgiving place, especially to anyone who does not respect what nature can dish out to the ill-prepared. In the fall of 1999, my Dad and I traveled to King Salmon, Alaska to close up or "winterize" Camp Brewer.

On a lark, Dad and I took a flight to Brooks Lodge. When we departed for Brooks, sometime in the mid-morning hours, my Dad said he was surprised at the relative warmth of that October morning.

Later that day, a north wind began to blow and the temperature plummeted. By the end of the day, the temps were well below freezing. Five days later, everything began to freeze. A series of snow-storms passed through the Alaskan Peninsula from the cold, cold North.

It was at that point in the trip that my Dad coined a phrase I won't soon forget. He said, "Son, God may give you this paradise each summer, but it should be obvious to you that each year he is going to take it back." Clearly, Dad had opined that God did not want me or anyone else in this 'God's country' during the winter months!

It was with that premise that I treaded with trepidation when I put skis on the airplane and made a run at winter flying.

I started the trip in Wasilla with a stop at the local flight school. When I walked in the door of the musty 1940's hangar, the mechanic and the old-timer flight instructor looked me up and down, apparently sizing me up for what I am - a city slicker impersonating a bush pilot.

I approached them with the same attitude I approach most everything, "What you think of me is none of my business."

I glad-handed the boys and explained I had put skis on an otherwise perfectly good wheel plane and I was intending to follow the Iditarod mushers up the trail.

The instructor, who I will call Papa Amish, greeted me with a smile and said he would be glad to teach me to tackle skis and tame the taildragger.

Well, what I should say is that his LIPS were saying that, but his mind and eyes were saying, "Isn't the Superbowl going on right now for you people down in America? It would probably be much safer to put a pair of Gucci slippers on and have your third maid fetch you a latte!"

I tried to win the old boy over by explaining that I had over nine-hundred hours of bush flying in Alaska. He was not moved.

Oh well, for some reason I was not the least bit defensive. There was something about the old-timer that put me at ease. Some feature, as I stared at him incessantly, that seemed so very familiar. The more I looked at him, the more I realized that I had seen him before.

No, not seen him before, but rather, I knew him somehow.

Then it dawned on me! Bill looked exactly like my Dad (in the eyes and nose) with an Amish beard.

I thought, "Hell, I can't think of a better symbol to attack winter flying than with an instructor that looks like Dad with a bad beard!"

It didn't take much to coerce 'Papa Amish' into the plane. He was the type of guy, an addict really, that would fly anything, anywhere. I knew the type. I AM the type. I am fond of Ugashik Bob's motto: "Anything worth doing is worth overdoing," especially when it comes to aviation.

Papa Amish was going to crawl into the plane and 'teach' me to fly even if I told him he was going to have to pay me to let him!

So Papa Amish said he would get up at the crack of 10:00 AM to meet me for the first lesson in flying a tail dragger.

3/4/07: I showed up to meet Papa Amish at the hangar at 10:00 AM. "What? No Papa Amish?" Oh well, I decided to re-pack all the survival gear. Papa Amish showed up a bit later and we pushed the plane out of the hangar. As we got outside I was confronted by what I had suspected I was in for.... bitter cold. I had neglected to put on my gloves, hat and a facemask. It was 25 degrees below outside and I felt like I had pushed the plane in to the world's biggest beehive and a thousand bees were attacking me!

I now had a new definition of cold. It was a very clear day, winds out of the west at 10-15 knots. No big deal as far as aviation was concerned, but brutal as far as I, the Southern California lawyer, was concerned.

Despite the icy bee stings, I completed a thorough pre-flight inspection of the plane, beyond what I had done inside the hangar and I jumped inside the cockpit beside Papa Amish.

I fired the plane up and taxied for Runway 24. Just like the seaplane, I horsed back on the yoke to keep the tail down.

As I turned into the wind to initiate the take-off roll, I felt like I was "coming home." I slowly advanced the throttle, the tail of the plane came up and she leaped off the runway.

Yes, this was a good feeling indeed. Light winds, clear skies, tires and skis. What more could a pilot want?

Papa Amish and I agreed that we should flight-test the engine for half an hour to determine whether it was road ready for the Iditarod and the adventures to come.

Regrettably, she was running rough all morning due to the cold temperatures. We stayed close to good landing spots which, in Alaska, is pretty much everywhere there is flat ground. Well, maybe not great to land on, but safe enough to make a survivable landing.

We made several touch-and-goes (practice take-offs and landings) on a hard-surfaced runway with the wheels down and the skis up. I complained to Papa Amish that I had had enough of city flying, so we headed over to Goose Bay for landings on a snow covered, gravel runway. I wanted to try out my new airplane skis. I turned my downwind leg in preparation to land which took us out over the Cook Inlet. At that time of day, the incoming tide had brought in icebergs the size of cars and buses - an awesome and intimidating sight! I kept my altitude on the downwind leg in case the engine betrayed Papa Amish and me.

As I set up for landing over the ice-encrusted Cook Inlet on my final approach for landing to the north, I checked the windsock to ensure we were approaching the runway from the appropriate direction. There was no breeze. A feather could have safely floated to the runway if you had dropped it from the center of the airfield.

When we were on short final, I ran the checklist one more time. As we descended through the tree-tops that surrounded the edges of the runway, the wings rocked violently and Papa Amish and I both hit our heads on the ceiling!

Papa Amish said, "Where the heck did that come from?" As we dropped over the runway, the wind continued to toy with us like a yo-yo on a string. I held the plane six inches off the runway until we could get the wind and the motor in agreement with the wings.

When everything stopped fighting and the wind calmed, I slowed the motor and the wings straightened out. The skis kissed the snow beneath me and we had joyfully defied gravity like never before.

I say 'never before' because it was the first time I had the pleasure of putting a pair of skis down on a snow-covered runway.

And then I said, "Cool!" That's all I could think to say before sliding my boots onto the brakes to slow the plane down. As I put my feet onto the brakes and gently pushed down, I realized that the plane was not slowing down! Out of habit, really, I pushed harder. I think the speed of the airplane actually increased a little bit.

Although it hadn't occurred to me when the skis touched the snow that a ski plane does not have brakes, I soon realized that I was simply along for the ride. And what a ride it was! I used the repetitive expression, "Cool."

Just like a ten-year-old boy on Space Mountain at Disneyland, I wanted to do that again and again and again! And so we did!

When the white needle on the gas gauge touched the 'E,' we headed over to Palmer Airport for some 'cheap blue gas' (aviation fuel is blue).

Palmer sits at the base of The Chugach Mountains. The Tazlina, Knik and several other glaciers surround the mountains. Palmer has a reputation of being a very windy place.

When we were about five miles south of the airport, I contacted the flight service station to apprise them of our position and intention to land. A lady from the flight service station said, in a pleasant voice, "Wind calm, use the longer north-south runway. No reported traffic." We set up for a landing to the south. As we made the turn to final, we experienced a severe crosswind. Something was wrong! All we could see out of the windows of the plane were huge glaciers! The crosswinds had turned our plane completely sideways and we had to look out the co-pilot's window to see the runway! Papa Amish said, once again, "Where the heck did that come from?" I apprised the lady from the flight service station that we were going to reestablish ourselves for a landing on the east runway due to the severe crosswind. She replied, "Yes, the wind picked up out of nowhere from the east." We landed uneventfully as the wind was blowing straight down Runway 9, the east facing runway.

As I jumped out of the plane and approached the fuel pumps, the wind shifted again! This time it was coming from the north, and the velocity increased again to 30 knots.

Aside from being awed by the constant shift in the wind direction, I was again shocked at how the biting cold first hurt and then numbed your face.

We refueled the plane and as we taxied out the wind shifted yet again. This time to the north. In

my experience, this sudden and potentially ominous shift of winds only occurs in Alaska. The young woman from the flight service station taunted us by saying, "You can depart from the runway intersection because I'll bet you can't turn that taildragger around in this wind."

We departed, hovered really, to the north, and Papa Amish suggested that we head for Skwentna and practice another ski landing. I was excited by the proposition of landing at Skwentna because this particular village is one of the early checkpoints on the Iditarod trail.

The mountains between Wasilla and Skwentna were unbelievable. Some may describe these mountains as majestic and beautiful, but believe me when I say that the size and majesty of the glaciers between Palmer and Skwentna took my breath away. I could see all the way to Talkeetna and beyond. Denali, the highest point in North America, was so close, I felt like I was sitting in the front row at the movie theater. You don't have to get too close to a 23,000-foot mountain to gain that sensation!

As we landed at Skwentna I again horsed down on the brakes in a vain attempt to slow the plane down. We slid aimlessly toward the end of the runway. I realized, at that point, that I could control the direction but not the speed of the plane.

After we landed in Skwentna, Papa Amish suggested that we take a break to stretch our legs. The 'terminal' at the Skwentna Airport is a sight to behold. It looks like a shipping container sitting on stilts, sided with wood, with a door and windows. I took a picture of the terminal at the airport in Skwentna. Papa Amish and I decided to call it a day and we headed back to Wasilla.

That night I did my day in review. As I looked at the photograph I had taken of the terminal at Skwentna, I saw him in the window: The Ghost of Skwenta. When you look closely at the window, you can see what appears to be an Alaskan native peering back at you. In my day, when we took pictures we had them developed at the local photo shop. The photo shop would deliver the photos to us, which included a series of negatives. In film photography a negative is an image, usually on a strip or sheet of transparent plastic film, in which the lightest areas of the photographed subject appear darkest and the darkest areas appear lightest. If you wanted to get additional copies of any given photograph you would take the negative back to the photo shop and they would use the negative to generate a duplicate photograph. If you look at the photograph I took of the terminal at the Skwentna Airport, where the image of the Alaskan Native appears, you have to view the window as if it's a negative, so the image of the Ghost of Skwentna is reversed. His face appears in the darkest area, and what would typically be considered to be the darkest areas, such as his hair, appear the lightest.

   As I put my head on the pillow that night, I thought about the Ghost of Skwentna, the ominous glaciers, the indecisive winds, the biting cold and the lack of braking authority of a ski plane. I went to sleep feeling like a very small man in a great wilderness. I felt like there was very little a mere mortal like me could do to control the direction of things that happen in the winter in Alaska.

   The next set of events that passed through my mind defies explanation. For some reason we had decided to take a drive in the country. You must be thinking, "Isn't Alaska remote enough that it already IS the country?!" in an old Ford Explorer. After a short drive up a very rocky mountain road we happened upon a tall, thin, gray-haired, gray-bearded German hiker. I will call him 'German Friend.' The old fellow was carrying an alder branch, utilizing same as his hiking stick. He was more than a day's hike away from town, and I had to wonder why he did not have a backpack or other means to keep himself viable. There were other aspects of my thoughts that did not make sense. My German Friend was wearing a short-sleeved shirt, short pants, and was standing in knee-deep green, very green, grass. Remember, Chap, it's the middle of winter in Alaska.

   As we rolled our Explorer up the road, my German Friend stepped off the side of the road and onto the tall green grass. As we pulled up along the side of German Friend, I rolled down the window and German Friend gave me a most welcome smile. He was obviously a warmhearted, earth-lovin' and people-lovin' kind of soul.

We engaged in the typical pleasant opening conversation. Just shy of a minute into the conversation a flash of something shiny and brown crossed my field of vision, then a second flash, followed by a third, much larger flash. As I turned my head and changed my focus, I realized that the third, larger figure was a large, agitated grizzly bear sow. The two smaller figures were her two young cubs. All three bears were huffing and barking, obviously distressed by having happened upon the three of us.

As quickly as the bears appeared, they disappeared, and suddenly reappeared. Apparently, Momma Bear was not happy that she was the one expected to take the kids and leave the grassy playground.

She responded by making a charge, head down, at German Friend. German Friend did not hesitate in giving ground, and he ran for the top of a small grass filled berm. Momma Bear stood on her hindquarters and looked for the cubs, then she made a run for GERMAN FRIEND.

Both Momma Bear and German Friend were out of sight for a few seconds. Somehow, German Friend found his way back to the Explorer before Momma Bear discovered his whereabouts. I had since crawled from the front passenger seat to the rear set of seats for a better view. As German Friend came towards the Explorer, so did the two cubs. I was certain that where the cubs appeared, Momma Bear was sure to follow. I threw open the back door to allow German Friend a means to escape Momma Bear's imminent charge. German Friend, for some inexplicable reason, still held his hiking stick in his right hand. He held onto that darned stick like a Mormon holding the Book of Mormon! As a result of the length of the stick, German Friend could not get through the open doorway.

Just at that instant, Momma Bear reappeared on the scene, and German Friend made a second run for the hills. I was about as scared as I could be; given the fact that the back door of the car was wide open. To my surprise, Momma Bear continued her pursuit of German Friend and followed him over a small incline. Momma Bear was out of sight for a few seconds.

Relieved that Momma Bear had not taken advantage of my vulnerability, I promptly pulled the back door closed. I started to say a brief prayer for German Friend, but before I could get to "Amen" a very large and angry Momma Bear crashed into the side of the truck, crushing in the side window. She continued to pound on the side of the truck for a few seconds. I sat in the back seat, amazed, and tried to figure out why Momma Bear would attack an innocent American-made truck when she had a perfectly good German tourist to pick on?

Speaking of German Friend, he reappeared back on the scene during Momma Bear's attempt to open the window from the outside of the car. Luckily for us, but not for German Friend, the chaos subsided when Momma Bear turned her attention again to German Friend. They both disappeared over the grassy ridge.

As I sat in the back seat in a state of shock, I contemplated why Momma Bear had attacked the truck. I eventually turned to my right to find I had a small, furry, brown companion sitting on the seat next to me.

I surmised that during German Friend's attempt to gain access to the back door of the truck, having left it open, the young cub had slid into the truck without either of us noticing.

I quickly opened the back door and pushed the cub out, but before I could get the door closed, I woke up from the dream straight out of Bear Hell.

I sat up in bed, in a pool of sweat, trying to catch my breath. I lay awake in bed for an hour or so, trying to make sense of why I had had such a vivid and three-dimensional dream.

I am reluctant to be terribly theatrical or philosophical, but maybe my Dad's words had proven to be prophetic. As Dr. Freud would say, maybe my psyche was trying to tell my small citified mind that "God had taken Alaska back for the winter, and a city-slicker like me had no place in nature."

In the dream, I was safely tucked away in an American-made metal cocoon, and nature had found its way inside the cocoon. The message seemed to be, "Lance, you can do all the flight testing you want; put all your survival gear in a neatly organized bag, and prepare all you want. But all the preparation in the world is not going to make a difference should I, Mother Nature, decide otherwise."

I woke up Sunday morning feeling challenged. If I did not understand before I dozed off the night before, I now had a complete understanding of the rules. I also had a renewed commitment to follow all the rules to ensure I would gain any possible advantage, should things not go as planned. If nothing else, I would continue to be prepared.

The message of the dream was reinforced by the weather that day. I woke up to wind. Big wind. It was blowing 40 knots from the north, gusting to 70 knots in the mountain passes. There would be no flight training today.

CHAPTER 10

A Trip to Anchorage

I RENTED A CAR and drove to Los Anchorage to pick up Harry and, of course, more supplies. I wanted Harry as my companion on this trip for three reasons. First, he is a trusted friend. Second, Harry is an outstanding mechanic. Third, he is a retired musher with a keen ability to survive in the outdoors.

I woke up this morning and asked myself the question most commonly asked by people visiting Alaska. "What day is it?" That is the beauty, the point really, of life in Alaska. Who cares what day it is?! Today is March 6, 2007. It's a Monday or a Tuesday. Today, Harry and I start the Iditarod Adventure.

Although it is 20 degrees below zero this morning I don't have a worry in the world because the plane is sitting in a heated hangar under the control of Papa Amish. We rechecked the plane, repacked our survival gear, and pushed the ski plane out of the hangar and into the cold, very cold, air. I realized we were asking plenty from the ski plane.

As with most airplanes, the ski plane is equipped with an air-cooled engine. In other words, as air flows over the engine, the air keeps the ski plane from overheating. A car, for example, relies on cold water from the radiator to keep the engine cool and to prevent it from overheating.

When we fly our planes in places like California or Arizona, down in America, we fly in relatively warm air. In such a warm environment we count on the opening in the front of the engine compartment, or cowling, to allow cool air to flow over the engine. So as the airflow and the cool air coming off the propeller flows over the engine, it cools the engine.

Unlike California, however, the air in Alaska is extremely cold. Especially today. It was only 20 degrees below zero in still air. The question I had to ask myself was, "How cold will that engine get when I accelerate the plane to 120 knots?" The large opening in the front of the engine that I relied upon

for cooling while flying in warm air was no friend to me or the ski plane during the winter months in Alaska. Oh well. We would find out soon enough. We fired up the engine on the ski plane and headed to the fuel pumps for some blue gas.

In Alaska, you can leave your American Express card behind. The MasterCard, or 'Masterblaster' as I like to call it, is what it's all about. I passed my Masterblaster through the credit card machine at the fuel pump and - NOTHING. I guess the credit card machine did not like the 20 below zero temperature reading we were getting that morning either. The local 'airport rat' came over to inquire about, well, everything. He asked, in a single phrase, "What kind of plane is it...was it always a tail dragger...how big is the engine...how fast, high, low, slow, will it go?"

After I answered all of his riveting questions, I asked the 'airport rat' if I could buy fuel at another nearby location, using the Masterblaster of course. He said, "Willa," which I understood to be Willow, Alaska, an airport located 36 miles to the north. As luck would have it, Willow is the start of this year's Iditarod. Although Wasilla is touted as being the city known as the "Start of the Iditarod," the restart took place in Willow because Wasilla lacked sufficient snow for the Mushers and their dog teams.

I did not mind taking a short flight to Willow, aka 'Willa,' as this would be an opportunity to determine whether the opening in the front of the engine allowed too much cool air to flow over the engine. We started the engine, made a standard departure from Wasilla and climbed through 2000 feet above ground level. As we climbed to a higher altitude, the oil temperature climbed just "into the green" or just into a temperature range that is acceptable to the fellas that designed the engine.

You see, as the ski plane or any other airplane climbs, the pilot is asking the most of the engine. The act of causing an airplane to climb is like driving a car up a hill, you are asking the most that engine can give. As a consequence, the engine is most likely to overheat during a climb uphill. However, I had never flown a plane in winter at temperatures approaching 20 below zero. What would the ski plane do when we leveled off at 3000 feet above the ground? At that point in the flight I would be

demanding less of the engine, creating less heat. But conversely, the outside air temperature was dropping as we climbed to the higher altitudes. The large opening in the front of the cowling had become our enemy. Our strength in the summer had become our weakness in the winter.

As we leveled off, the temperature of the oil plummeted to the minimum acceptable level. We needed to remedy the situation in Willow by reducing the amount of cold air being allowed access to the engine. We reduced our power setting and pulled the power way back so that we could descend towards Willow. As we reduced power, we made less heat. I feared the engine would not run well or even quit running altogether.

When we landed at Willow, we decided that the best way to reduce the amount of cold air flowing into the engine compartment would be to put Duct Tape over the air inlets to the engine. That's right, we put '100 mph tape' over one-half of the front cowling. We also covered the oil cooler with another type of tape - foil tape. We figured that if we would restrict the amount of cold air getting into the engine compartment we could keep the ski plane warm. I also had a sick curiosity regarding whether the '100 mph' tape would hold up to speeds well exceeding 100 mph!

After the refueling and taping sessions were complete, we headed for McGrath, Alaska, via the Rainy Pass. I had already stopped at Skwentna the preceding day, so I mostly knew my way towards Rainy Pass. It was, as we like to say in aviation, a "Blue Bird" day. In other words, it was very clear as we flew towards Rainy Pass. The air was smooth, which is important, considering that Harry has a propensity to regurgitate his breakfast in a plastic bag during about every flight. That's right; Harry was embarking on 25 hours of his dream vacation which involves, mostly, throwing up each meal.

I can't imagine why he loves to fly so much. He gets airsickness almost every time we go flying. Nice vacation!

As we climbed to 8500 feet, the engine responded to our kindness by developing the necessary heat

and power to run in the low half of the green arch, or well into the acceptable temperature range. The cylinder-head temperatures followed in kind.

As we approached Rainy Pass, it was white in all directions, as far as the eye could see. Glaciers surrounded us, and the ground was as pretty as it was unwelcoming.

It was at this point that I turned my attention from piloting to mushing. I realized, perhaps for the first time, that the Iditarod is not a series of short mushing trips, with intermittent stops for food and camping.

As I looked down at the unforgiving land, I noticed the wind was gusting to well above 40 knots. What was it like for the dog mushers and their teams? How much pain would they endure in the name of competition? These were, as you and I like to say, "manly men doing manly things." I jest when I say that because history has taught us that there are some very hardy women on the trail tackling the same feat, often better than the men. Female mushers have outdone their male counterparts with some frequency. DeeDee Jonrowe and Libby Reynolds, among others, have won The Last Great Race. We come from families with strong women so we have to applaud this accomplishment with vigor.

The thought of the strength of the mushers and their teams was interrupted by my debate with Harry over "which way we need to head to get to the Rainy Pass." Harry had his finger on the chart (map), while I was cheating by using the GPS. It seems the GPS did not like the extremely cold weather and decided to take a break. Thank God for Harry's finger. Before I left home, you may remember, I had played with the computer on Iditarod.com. As I toyed with the mapping programs then, I was able to fly through the Rainy Pass using the 3D technology. Now, as I was heading towards it, I said, "That's no pass - it's the maze from the movie The Shining."

I coddled the GPS as Harry drew a line towards Nikolai with his finger. The combination, plus lots of altitude, allowed for a safe trip to the Nikolai checkpoint. As we passed over the river in front of the checkpoint we noted the extreme winds. We elected to avoid a landing on what appeared to be a sometimes windblown, sometimes icy river and play it safe by heading directly to the hard-surfaced runway at McGrath.

Upon our arrival at McGrath, we set up for a landing on the north-facing runway into a stiff 30 plus knot wind. The wind was blowing right down the runway, so landing the taildragger was not a problem. Well, I should say no problem for landing the plane, but a big problem for the pilot when he left the plane and attempted to tie her down.

Unlike flying down in America, the snow-covered airports in Alaska are not always user friendly. We taxied the ski plane up to what appeared to be a parking spot with a tie-down. This would normally be a spot with hard points in the ground to which we could attach our ropes to secure the ski plane. When we removed the snow-covered ground, there were no anchors to which to secure the plane. So, we had to move the plane to another spot.

Let me tell you, moving a plane by hand in a 30-knot wind is a challenge, but moving a plane in that kind of wind when the outside air temperature is well below zero is almost more than I could handle. After we tied the ski plane down, we made our way into the office of a local FBO or Fixed Base Operator and asked if we could use the telephone to call the Bed and Breakfast. It was not really an office. It was more like four telephone booths strapped together, walls removed. I asked the pilot on duty if I could borrow the telephone. He said, "Sure, but before you do, you had better put your hand over your nose to warm it up, your nose is completely white with frostbite."

Oddly, I did not recall feeling any pain in or around my nose. In fact, I had not even felt my nose since I crawled out of the plane and pushed the ski plane across the tarmac to the new parking spot.

In any event, the telephone for the B & B rang off the hook. Harry and I had to hoof it up the road to the B & B. Before heading up the road to the B&B, we had to put the ski plane to bed. In order to avoid the inevitable return to the airport to find the ski plane encased in ice, it is necessary to cover the wings, front cowl and tail feathers before departing the airport. We had no choice in the matter. If Harry and I neglected the ski plane we would spend the entire following morning scraping the ski plane until it was completely free of ice. Let's face it, ice cubes don't fly worth a darn. So, to avoid the pain of scraping ice, we completely covered the ski plane.

When we arrived at the B&B, we received the news that we would be sharing our room with four other people. The B&B was located a couple of hundred yards away from the Iditarod Checkpoint, so after dinner we made our way down to the checkpoint. On a normal day the checkpoint serves as a school building, but during The Last Great Race, the school is transformed into a rest stop for dogs and mushers, housing for media, logistical headquarters for the Iditarod Airforce, etc. The building sits just along the Kuskokwim River. Hence, the dog teams leave the flats of the icy river, follow a road to the checkpoint, and depart by heading back down to the river.

A crowd was gathering around the checkpoint in anticipation of the arrival of the first-place musher. After having flown over the foggy, windy, ice-laden Rainy Pass, I cannot imagine what the Mushers and their pups had endured in coming over the Rainy Pass. When they started the Race, they began at an elevation close to sea level. The teams had to pull the musher and the loaded sled to the top of Rainy Pass, some 3160 above sea level. Those dogs must have some pulling power. Can you imagine your dog and fourteen of his friends pulling you up 3000 feet? Tough going, to be sure.

From the reports we had received, and what we witnessed from the air, the pass was brutally windy. Apparently, many of the teams had elected to hole up in Rainy Pass. We were hearing rumors that with the near hurricane-force winds, one musher missed a turn going to Rainy Pass and instead followed the trail to Ptarmigan Pass. You might remember that during preparation for this trip, I considered the option of flying the wider, more welcoming Ptarmigan Pass. It must look considerably different while traveling the route on the ground and at least one musher has become confused and traveled down onto the South Fork Kuskokwim River. Either trail will take the team to the checkpoint in Rohn, but the distance through the pass through the South Fork is considerable. Easier said than done. The outside air temperature was 20 to 30 below zero, not taking into account the wind chill factor.

As I looked down at the Kuskokwim River, it appeared that there was water running over the river ice for a seven- to ten-mile stretch. If a dog team were to mistakenly attempt to cross the river at that location, it would be chaos trying to get the team untangled. Further, if the Musher had the misfortune of getting dragged into the water by his or her dog team it would be difficult for a waterlogged musher to recover from the frostbite.

As evidence of the brutality of the weather conditions in Rainy Pass consider that by the time the mushers reached Rainy Pass, thirteen teams had scratched. Two of the teams that withdrew from the race were former Iditarod champions. One such champ, Doug Swingley, broke his ribs and right thumb when he fell off his sled. Another famous musher, Dee Dee Jonroe, lost control of her sled on the ice coming off the pass. Both of the mushers reported that they were concerned for the well-being of their dog teams if they attempted to continue the race so they put the well-being of the dogs ahead of their ambition. Pretty noble.

The first musher and dog team to arrive at the Mc-Grath Checkpoint was Martin Buser. It is so odd to be at a checkpoint. Do you remember when you were a kid and I use to take you to the California Angel's baseball games? During the course of most professional baseball games the manager of the team has to go out to the pitcher's mound to have a discussion with a struggling pitcher. As I watched this event unfold at the baseball

game, I was often curious about the manner and substance of those conversations! At the Iditarod checkpoints the mushers, race officials, vets, media, and fans all huddle right next to the musher upon their arrival at the checkpoint. It feels as though you are welcome to stand on the pitcher's mound in the middle of a game in the heat of a discussion between a pitching coach and ailing pitcher.

You can, and I did, ask the mushers any question you wanted. The first musher, Martin Buser asked me to step on his snow anchor and hold his dog sled at the station temporarily. I was transformed from fan to participant in a matter of seconds. The then-leader of the race, Martin Buser, explained to me that while he was coming over the Rainy Pass "I fell off my sled on a patch of ice. I think it was the location where all the mushers are having a hard time. I lost my sled and the team continued on without me. Luckily, she," pointing at a female second in line, "is in heat and he, pointing at his leader, can't keep his paws off of her. So, my lead dog turned to get at her and the ropes got all balled up. I ran down the trail, caught the dogs due to the tangle, and here I am in first place. A little luck sure goes a long way on a race like this."

It was exciting and refreshing to be a witness to spontaneous, reactive statements. Martin was very friendly. I think he told me that he has run the Iditarod 22 times and has won the race 4 times. Only Martin Buser and Jeff King have won the Iditarod 4 times. At one point I said, "I bet you could run this race blind-folded?" Martin responded in a tired but excited tone, "I think you are right there."

The next morning Harry and I returned to the ski plane and started the morning regimen. It starts with uncovering the ski plane and attempting to fold snow crusted frozen covers. The morning tem-

peratures were around 20 degrees below zero. As the temps approach 20 below zero, you have to be very careful. If you take off your gloves to do anything, your hands will pay a price. If you do not have a means to warm up your hands, the pain will be with you for the remainder of the day. The cold can get so bad, so quick, that your hands feel like you have a sunburn.

Oh, yeah, the ski plane. After the covers are off the ski plane, with the exception of the cowl cover (thick blanket over the front hood and propeller), the engine must be pre-heated. Lighting what appears to be a torch under the engine compartment and stuffing an exhaust tube up into the engine compartment completes this task. Since the torch is effectively an open flame and is placed next to the gas/fuel drain, a warmly dressed co-pilot must guard the open flame with a fire extinguisher. I am only allowed to BBQ one plane a year, and with the loss of Juliet Yankee I am more diligent than the average volunteer fire fighter.

Like I said, at 20 below zero it takes around two hours to warm the engine and oil to the point that it is safe to attempt an engine start. After the engine starts, it takes up to twenty minutes to warm the engine to the point that you can attempt to complete a pre-flight run up. In sum, you don't want to be in a hurry as a winter flyer. Everything takes time, and if you learn nothing else from winter flying in Alaska, you learn patience. And to overdress for the occasion.

Basically, Harry and I concluded that it was necessary to be at the plane by 7:00 AM if we wanted to depart by 9:30 AM. On that first morning in McGrath, Harry and I spent the first couple of hours getting the ski plane ready for the warm up. After getting the plane preheated, and re-packing our emergency gear, we crawled into the refrigerated cockpit and I turned the key in anticipation of the morning roar from the engine - NOTHING - CLICK - NOTHING. Apparently, unlike Elvis Presley (he lives in Mexico, you know), the battery was completely dead.

So, we quickly put the cowl cover back on the engine so that we could preserve the heat we had created with the Northern Companion torch. We then took everything out of the back of the well-packed plane to gain access to the inconveniently located battery that is sitting behind the rear bulkhead. After

removing 24 screws from the bulkhead, we inspected the battery and discovered that the brain-donor of a mechanic that had signed an annual inspection the preceding week had neglected to do the requisite maintenance on the battery. The leads were badly corroded and the battery was nearly dry. This, my son, is an unforgivable sin. No self-respecting aviation maintenance professional sends a plane, pilot and passengers into the arctic winter with an unserviced battery. The battery, or the lack thereof, could literally be the death of you.

But, where would we find battery acid in McGrath, Alaska? There were two things I noted the village needed upon our arrival: First, a dentist. You may know the pick-up line in Alaska, "Hi honey, nice tooth." Second, a self-respecting aircraft mechanic with a hangar filled with sundries: perhaps battery acid. We were done for the day, maybe more. We spent the entire day trying to find either acid or a healthy battery, lest we spend the better part of the winter in McGrath, Alaska.

Lucky for us, the owner of the B&B had a pint of acid left over, and that was just enough to fill the battery and attempt a re-charge. After three hours of charging, we attempted a start and, thanks be to God, we had enough cranking power to get the engine going. That was good news indeed. The bad news was that we would have to take the battery out of the back of the plane after each flight, keep it warm and re-charge it each night. So goes life in bush Alaska - especially in the winter months. We took the ski plane for a test flight, which I will tell you about in a bit, and we tucked her in for the evening.

McGrath was over-flowing with people that evening. Most of the people in the crowd were race volunteers, including pilots from the Iditarod air force. Also, each major local television station has at least three people in the village to cover the event.

The first evening Harry mentioned that he was surprised that the major TV networks had sent so many people to cover the event. He went on to describe a quite attractive young anchorwoman, Megan Baldino, in some detail. Harry ended his adjective-filled diatribe saying, "Wouldn't it be funny if

Megan was assigned to cover the Iditarod from McGrath? She's cute!"

As we meandered towards the checkpoint on the Kuskokwim River we noticed a set of very bright lights. As we approached, it was apparent that the Channel 2 news team was in the midst of a live telecast. The young anchorwoman was none other than Harry's dream girl, Megan Baldino. Harry blushed in amazement.

I teased my shy friend and tried to get him to approach her so I could take a picture. But our strong and gentle friend was not about to get within one-hundred feet of Megan. It was as though Harry was a stalker, the subject of a well-drafted restraining order, preventing him from getting within one-hundred feet of her. No way!

That night, we greeted several mushers and their dog teams. At each stop, in addition to feeding the dogs, the mushers replace each dog's booties. A bootie is a set of four small nylon boots that are worn by each dog to protect their paws from wearing on the ice, rocks and other obstacles. Like a foul ball at a baseball game, the booties are a prize to Iditarod fans. Some of the mushers would toss the booties to the fans as they removed them from the dogs. That evening, I was the fortunate recipient of a single bootie. I handed the bootie to Harry as a gift to Harry's boy, Gregory.

We continued to make the rounds through the Iditarod checkpoint, eventually getting so cold we decided to seek refuge in the school building. After we warmed up for a bit we wandered through the building and happened upon the media room. The media room houses all of the equipment and personnel from the newspapers and TV stations.

As luck would have it (at least as far as Harry is concerned) Megan Baldino was in the media room rehearsing her lines for the next segment of the 10 o'clock news. I passed through and said "hello" to Megan and her crew, making some smart comment, and mentioned that my friend from Naknek is a big fan of Megan's. I introduced Megan to Harry, who, naturally, was speechless. We made small

talk with Megan for a few minutes and Megan inquired if we knew where she could get a set of dog booties for the next segment of the newscast, as she needed them as a prop. Well, Harry chimed right in, dangling the prized bootie, he indicated he had just such a bootie that Megan could borrow. However, the bootie was intended to be a keepsake for his young son, but that he would be happy to donate it to the Channel 2 News team for a few minutes.

Harry continued to make pleasant conversation with Megan as he handed her the bootie. We hung around the media filled room as the reporters practiced their lines, film crews worked on their cameras, producers talked on satellite phones and everyone joined in conversation which involved mostly making jokes and exchanging barbs. After several minutes Harry and I headed towards the back door. Megan saw Harry making what appeared to be an early departure and, interrupting the rehearsal of other news crews she yelled, "Hey Harry, aren't you gonna stick around for the bootie?"

Jaws dropped. The room went quiet, very quiet. Harry said, blushing, "I'm always willing to wait for my bootie," at which point Megan realized that she had blurted out a classic double entendre and the room broke out abruptly in laughter.

The story has a happy ending inasmuch as Harry recaptured his, not Megan's, bootie and he returned to the B&B with a story that is frequently revisited and repeated. I am sure Nomers will have heard the story by daybreak, given the speed of what Ugashik Bob refers to as the Tundra Telegraph.

The following morning Harry and I trudged our way through the morning snowstorm to the airport, battery in tow, completing our morning regimen of preheating the ski plane in robotic fashion. It was difficult to attempt to turn the key of the ski plane while holding my fingers crossed, but as I turned the key the engine cranked over and the front end of the ski plane was noisy once again. We headed for Unalakleet.

When we departed McGrath it was 20 degrees below zero, snowing lightly in relatively calm winds. You could almost make out blue sky through the light overcast. I would estimate the distance between

McGrath and Unalakleet, at least based on our intended routing, to be around 220 miles. Unalakleet is located right on the coast, on the Norton Sound. As the Norton Sound opens up, it becomes the Bering Sea. Just across the street, Russia. I asked a local if he had ever seen a polar bear in that part of Alaska. He laughed at me as though I had asked him if he lived in an igloo and said, "You have to go much further north for the white bears."

Our plan of attack, insofar as the day of flying was concerned, was to fly down the valley towards Takotna, a checkpoint famous for pies made for the mushers – (no, not Eskimo Pies), on to Ophir and over to the village of Iditarod. Yes, Iditarod is actually the name of a village in Alaska. We would land on the river in Iditarod and then depart for Unalakleet. As we departed McGrath, the snowstorm relented a bit, patches of blue sky appeared intermittently, and we had high hopes of an effortless trip to Unalakleet.

We made our way approximately 30 miles into the valley and a layer of light fog and low clouds surrounded the checkpoint in Takotna. We made a circle around the airport and then the river, noting that the Iditarod Airforce had made a ski landing on the river to drop off volunteers at the checkpoint. We gathered this information by tuning our aircraft radio to 120.6, which is the frequency used by the Iditarod Airforce while traveling on the Iditarod trail. By listening on 120.6, we had access to a wealth of information, from weather and landing conditions, to rumors of the locations and success of each team.

As we peered down the valley towards Ophir and Iditarod, it was clear that it was not clear. An area of fog and low clouds blocked the way to our destination. We turned the plane towards a low-level pass on course to Unalakleet. No joy. The same stubborn band of moisture blocked this pass. We picked our way through another pass slightly off our intended course to Unalakleet. No luck there, either. Contrary to popular opinion, the third time is not always a charm and the visibility continued to decline.

The next option was to retreat to McGrath, find the blue sky, climb into it, and travel to Unalakleet above the clouds, fog and mountains.

It took a bit to get the heavily loaded Cessna to 10,500 feet, but we found clear blue air and headed towards the Norton Sound. We crossed the Yukon River and continued over low-lying mountains just east of Unalakleet. When we had the icebergs in the Norton Sound in sight, we started our slow descent. As I very slowly brought the engine power back, like I was milking a mouse, it was apparent that the engine

stopped making heat and the temperature inside the cockpit dropped to well below zero. I felt like a side of beef hanging inside a walk-in freezer. A strange, but new, winter flying experience.

As mentioned previously, Unalakleet rests directly on the coast; surrounded by low level, two-to three-thousand foot hills, not really mountains, considering Denali and all. The coastal area in which the village sits is predictably flat. The ocean immediately in front of the village is frozen solid for approximately one-half a mile, where the ice collides violently with the incoming tide and very large icebergs mark the beginning of the tide-line. It takes extremely cold temperatures to freeze salt water. I watched various locals hastily make tracks on their snow machines across the ice. Scary.

The process of putting the ski plane to bed each night was beginning to take on the feeling of "Ground Hog Day," but we did the deed and trudged our way across the frozen tarmac, Harry and I alternating the lugging of our pet battery. Regrettably, Megan the TV star had spied us removing the battery after each flight. So, she and her crew gave Harry and me the nicknames, "Click and Clack."

CHAPTER 11

The Post Card

IT'S MARCH 9. The outside air temperature was a warm minus 5 degrees. Luckily, Harry's friend, SealSkin Phil, had access to a newly remodeled apartment just off the airport. Phil's brother lives in Unalakleet and he provided us with the apartment. Our plan was to use Unalakleet as our home base for a few days. I was very excited to be in Unalakleet, because tomorrow is "Bobby" Day! In other words, tomorrow is the day I am supposed to fly from Unalakleet to Nome, to pick up Bobby. I haven't heard from him since I left California. Will he show up in Nome?

You might remember that I invited Bobby to join Harry and I on this trip up the trail to Nome. Today is the day to pick up Bobby in Nome. I wish I could say that today was like any other day, but it isn't. I went out to the ski plane early this morning to prepare the plane for the departure to Nome. It was 25 degrees below zero. I spent an hour preheating the engine with a torch under the plane. The entire time I was cussing Bobby. Actually, I was cussing myself. I had hatched an evil scheme well in advance of my trip to the Iditarod. You see, I didn't really think that Bobby was going to make the trip to Nome. Not that I don't love Bobby, I do. Bobby said he would make the trip with me, but in my heart I had my doubts, serious doubts. So much so that several months ago, on my last visit to Alaska, I borrowed a pair of snowshoes. I went to a frozen lake and asked a local pilot to take, a well-staged, picture of me standing in front of a ski-plane. This was several months before the Iditarod, so I had to take a staged picture to make it look like I was dressed for the Iditarod. When I returned home, I had the picture made into a post card. I was betting that Bobby was not going to make it to Alaska to fly the Iditarod with Harry and me. When I arrived in Anchorage a few days ago, I mailed the post card to Bobby, anticipating he would be a no-show, in the postcard I said: "Dude, you should be in Nome." If I guessed correctly, I am going to want a copy of that post card for your journal and Bobby will be eating crow tonight. We will see.

It's evening now: I was minutes away from completing the process of preheating the engine. I was ready to take the covers off the wings of the ski plane to go to Nome to retrieve Bobby when the satellite phone rang. I picked up the phone to hear the distant voice of my work-wife, Kathryn. Kathryn was breaking up, I could hardly hear what she was saying. It was as if she was talking to me on a vintage 1940's two-way radio. I could hear a frustrated Kathryn yelling to me. I yelled back to her. Finally, I could hear her screaming "Don't go to Nome, Bobby can't make it. Can you hear me? DON'T GO." I simply replied: "Understand, DON'T GO TO NOME." She replied, "We are good, then." I lost Kathryn. Just static, but still music to my ears! For the cost of a stamp, I will be spoon-feeding Bobby crow's meat, feathers and all, for time and all eternity.

With the loss of Bobby, our new plan was to travel east towards Koyuk, southeast towards Anvik and Eagle Island, to meet the mushers as they came up the Yukon River.

I was told to expect that for most of our visit in Unalakleet, that the wind would blow a persistent 30 knots out of the north, which was not a problem for us since the runway was facing north and south, as was our landing way on the snow-covered Yukon River. But for the mushers and their teams, it was a different story; they were taking a beating as they pushed directly into the wind as they made tracks heading north, up the mighty Yukon River. And so here we are safely in Unalakleet, the last major village before Nome.

A new day – although I would not swear to it, I am relatively certain that today is March 9 - a Friday. Our mission is to set off to Anvik, a village located on the Yukon. Today the winds are blowing 25 knots from the North, gusting with some frequency to 35 knots. You have to remember that every place north of here is cold, very cold, so the air being blown to us is chilly, very chilly.

I called the flight service station and obtained a weather briefing while Harry pre-heated the ski plane. Our pre-flight briefing had included a prayer by Harry for calm winds as we passed over the line of hills/mountains to the southeast. As we approached Anvik, the wind speed accelerated considerably.

The snow on the river in front of the village had drifted significantly which precluded the possibility that I could safely land on the river. As I listened on the radio frequency for the Iditarod Airforce, I heard several comments about aborted attempts to land at Anvik due to severe downdrafts and crosswinds. I presumed the pilots were talking about landing on the river, so we headed for the airport. The airport sits on a bluff and is surrounded by large, layered, trees. I thought "this could be really tricky" as the wind was "quartering the runway." I reported on the common traffic advisory frequency that I was "five miles north of the airport, making left traffic for the north runway."

A pilot responded that he had encountered severe downdrafts as he approached the runway at Anvik. As we made our turn to final to land on the north facing runway, I applied a single notch of flaps and maintained a higher than normal approach speed to account for the potential down draft. When the ski plane arrived at 100 feet above ground level the wings rocked violently, and Harry was staring at the ground from his vantage point on the right side of the plane. I increased power, retracted the flaps, put my tail between my legs and pointed the ski plane towards Shageluk. Shageluk is another Iditarod checkpoint, located just east of Anvik.

We completed several "fly-bys," alternating between the village, river and the airport, contemplating a landing on the river located just a few seconds by foot from the village. Again, the snow and ice on the river looked uninviting, despite the fact that two other brave pilots had found refuge on the river. I had guessed that it would be a two-mile walk from the airport to the village. As Grampa Auggie would say, "There are old pilots and there are bold pilots, but there are no old, bold pilots." I opted to be an 'old pilot' and headed for the airport.

The welcome mat was out at the airport as the wind was blowing 30 knots from the north at Shageluk, but right down the runway, making the landing a bit easier. I was not the only pilot looking for refuge in Shageluk. As we approached the village, five other airplanes were in the traffic pattern trying to find a calm place to call home. Of the five planes, two were able to land on the river; the remaining

three of us opted for the safety of the airport.

We landed and pondered the two-mile walk down the old village road in thirty-knot winds. The downwind walk, meaning with the wind, to the village was not so much of a problem. But the return venture into the wind coming back to the airport could be painful. We feared that we could get hypothermic, which was no longer a joking matter as far as I was concerned.

We threw caution to the wind and started our march downwind towards the village. We waltzed down the trail towards the village and, I know I called it a road, but it really was just wide enough for a single car. After walking approximately 1.8 miles, we realized that I had badly estimated the distance between the village and the airport. Fortunately, an old native woman passed by on a four-wheeler and offered us a ride to the village. The four-wheeler was of the small variety and the native woman was already carrying a single, oversized passenger. Given the choice, I decided I would prefer to die a swift death on a four-wheeler, rather than a slow death from hypothermia.

So, Harry and I climbed on the front and back of the now sagging four-wheeler. The elderly native woman apparently thought the throttle was an on/off switch, with a single setting. She turned the throttle to the "on" position as Harry, I and John Doe hung on for dear life as we headed for the village at Mach 5.

The village of Shageluk is small, very small, and yes, Harry and I arrived alive. The population is around one-hundred twenty-five people. A single team of dogs passed through the village. The musher informed the race volunteers that he intended to press on, the vets checked the dogs over for a couple of minutes and the team was through the village with the efficiency of an Indy 500 pit crew.

The next team was around one hour away from the village, so we elected to go to the village store, grab a snack and make our way back to the airport. Harry waved a $20 bill in the face of a local native man with a truck, converting the man from a local scrimshaw artist to an Iditarod Taxi Driver in a New York second. In Alaska, a New York Second is defined as the time that elapses between the second you wave a $20 in the face of the native versus the nano-second that elapses when the native grabs the $20 bill from your hand.

I hate four letter words, especially four-letter words that start with 'W!' Like 'Wind'. But, we departed the airport in a stiff 35-knot WIND, following the dog teams to the north up the Yukon. You might have guessed by now that all of the runways in this part of Alaska face north and south. If I were a betting man, I would bet the runways are orient-

ed pointing north because the prevailing winds come from the north. The dog teams would have to continue to trudge up the Yukon River with the wind directly in their furry faces. As we departed Shageluk, we looked down to see one such team struggling with the wind as they made their way up the Yukon. The musher, however, was in a tucked position like a downhill skier. I thought that was an interesting strategy to combat the wind. He or she would have to maintain the semi-squatting position for an extended period of time.

If you think about it, a musher is more like a long-distance runner that is sleep deprived. On several occasions during the race, I watched dog teams charge up slope, or uphill. As the teams started up the hill, the musher jumped off the sled to reduce the weight in the sled. The average dog team is traveling between 6 and 10 miles per hour. So, if a musher jumps off the sled the musher has to chase the sled at a pretty good clip!

The wind and ice were definitely taking a toll on the dog teams. As the race progressed, I noticed that the teams were getting smaller and smaller as we increasingly visited checkpoints. While the majority of the mushers started with fifteen dogs, many of the teams had dropped two or three dogs by McGrath, Iditarod and Shageluk.

If a dog is injured, or goes lame mid-trail, the musher and his dogteam pays the penalty twice. First, the dog team loses the pulling power of a mighty powerful little dog. I say little dog because as I approached the line of fifteen dogs for the first time the dogs appeared to me to be fifteen greyhounds with long hair. The second burden or penalty to the team: not only does the team lose the pulling pow-

er of the injured dog, but the Official Rules of the Iditarod require that the musher place the injured dog in his or her sled and take the dog to the next checkpoint. In that event, the team is forced to carry the additional 45 pounds of lame dog to the next village.

This can be problematic, depending on the point in the race at which the dog suffers the injury. If, for example, a dog were to lose a bootie and cut his paw on the ice a few miles outside a village, the musher could elect to turn back to the village.

The decision of whether to continue to the next checkpoint or turn back to the village is strategic, of course, depending upon the length of the leg between checkpoints. The shortest leg of this year's race is between Wasilla and Knik, fourteen miles. The longest distance between checkpoints is the barren land between Rohn and Nikoli, ninety-three long and lonely miles. Can you imagine the grumbling that goes on within the team when one of the dogs is placed in the basket and the rest of the gang has to carry an additional 45 pounds some ninety-three miles? If dogs could only talk!

To give you a point of reference, it takes a fast team of dogs over two hours to travel between Wasilla and Knik, which is the shortest distance between checkpoints. The distance between the village of Iditarod and Shageluk is sixty-five miles. It took one of the relatively fast dog teams over nine hours to travel that distance during the course of the current race. The team averaged 7.5 miles per hour.

I'll bet the team of dogs is relieved to drop the additional 45 pounds of dead weight, and they certainly must feel the difference after dropping off their disabled friend in the village and renew their attempt to drag the sled across the snow, ice and overflow. They may be thinking "Hmmm…now if we could just dump the musher, we could get to Nome in no time!" I would guess the frozen strips of moose meat serve as the musher's insurance that he makes it all the way to Nome.

During the stop in McGrath I had the opportunity to have a conversation with musher Cim Smith.

At that point, I think he was eight hours behind the leader. I asked Cim if he thought he was still in the game. Cim said, "I am very much alive, as anything can happen this early in the race." He and his team had traveled four-hundred thirty-six windy miles from Willow to McGrath. That portion of the trip included the treachery of the Rainy Pass. They had another six-hundred-fifty-three grueling miles before pulling into Nome. There was plenty of race to be run, enduring bad weather, dropped dogs, an injured musher, a strong headwind at the wrong point in the race. Any of these factors can make the difference in terms of hours or even days. "I am very much in the race," Cim exclaimed in a tired but resolute tone.

I can't emphasize enough how tired Cim sounded. Cim had covered the first four-hundred thirty-six miles of the race over a four-day period. I asked Cim how much sleep he had to that point in the race. He said, "I'm guessing nine hours total. Ya think that's enough?" I laughed and said, "My teenage son got eleven hours sleep last night." Cim responded with a polite chuckle.

It was at this checkpoint that I was hoping to get the opportunity to interact with 2004 Iditarod champion Mitch Seavey. If anyone in this race has the tenacity to challenge Lance Mackey, it's Seavey. Seavey is a true champion of the sport and comes by his 'take no prisoners' attitude honestly. He is the son of Dan Seavey, Sr., one of the founders of the Iditarod Dog Sled Race. Dan Seavey Sr., Joe Redington Sr., Tom Johnson and Gleo Huyck worked tirelessly to preserve the Iditarod National Historic Trail. Dan Seavey and Mitch Seavey will, no doubt, pass their knowledge and love for the sport on to the next generation. Surely, the legacy will continue beyond Dan and Mitch Seavey.

© Ugashik Bob 2015

CHAPTER 12

Time Is Broken

TODAY MUST BE SATURDAY - 3/10/07. We are trying to locate the lead dog teams and their mushers, as it is today's ambition to meet the top three dog teams as they enter each village. Today, there seems to be a difference of opinion between the pilot and co-pilot regarding our destination. Harry is committed to going all the way back to Iditarod. There are rumored to be artifacts in the "old village" of Iditarod. It was Harry's end and aim to get to Iditarod. I kid; of course, I would love to get there as well.

I was planning a ski landing on the river immediately in front of the village in Iditarod. I interrupted an old timer native pilot as he put his rifle in his airplane to ask if he had recently landed on the river in front of Iditarod. He said, "Yes, the landing area is on the river and it is marked with spruce boughs. With a north wind you will usually land up river toward the village." He continued with a monotone voice, "The landing area can be extremely rough due to the wind drifts and frozen overflow. If you taxi to the checkpoint stay away from the east side of the river bank, it is covered with overflow ice and there is an old tractor buried halfway in the ice."

I kidded with him and asked, "How long would it take to get there on a snow machine?" I added the obligatory native phrase, "I joke." In Alaska when a native says something he or she intends to be funny, especially a statement intended to be sarcasm, a good native will end with the phrase, "I joke." I love that Alaskan quirk.

So, if you find that your mind is wandering during a conversation with a native, all you have to do is laugh when you hear the phrase "I joke." It's Alaska's version of an "Applaud" sign at the Late Nite Show.

I thanked my native friend for his advice and inquired whether he was flying to the southeast, as were

we. He said, "No, my father and I are going to catch a caribou." Somehow, I don't think his goal was to "catch" a caribou. A man with a rifle is not intent on catching anything but a dirt nap, for the caribou, that is. No criticism here, as I had visited the local "supermarket" in each village. I did not see any fresh meat for sale. To my way of thinking, this was a village elder fixing to do some shopping. He and his family would be well served by his success.

Before he left, the native man asked if I would help his father hold his plane on the ice to keep it from sliding away. He needed to pick up some additional gas. He was worried his elderly father could not hold the plane alone on the ice by himself if the wind kicked up. He would just be a minute, as he needed to retrieve a couple of five-gallon jugs of gasoline he had stashed in the bushes. While I stood by his plane, his father and I exchanged pleasantries. A few minutes into the conversation the elderly native man said, "We have to go to the North Country to find caribou. In my day, we used to cross the river with dog sleds about twenty-five miles from here, but the river is wide-open water. It was too warm in February. It's hard to understand what the weather will do these days – time is broken."

My heart skipped a beat when he used the phrase, "Time is Broken" --- it stuck with me, so I wrote this poem.

TIME IS BROKEN

Time is broken — I am feeling the wrath
The ice is gone — it stole my path
The year is young — just 58 days
River should be frozen — the sky gray

Is it man — or is it God
Either way — this seems odd
I can't complete — my winter chores
I need food — there's no store

I can trade — my old pelts
But the hardship — will be felt
I'm not worried — I'll get by
But my grandson — for him I cry

After finishing taking into consideration what the local pilot said about the terrain and the condition of the river over at Iditarod, I reconsidered our options. The easy choice was to travel towards the more welcoming conditions over at Eagle Island. While eavesdropping on the Iditarod Airforce radio frequency the preceding day, I overheard an experienced pilot report to a rookie pilot that landing at Eagle Island was a "no brainer." I am all about having an equal number of takeoffs and landings in my logbook, so we headed for Eagle Island. The Iditarod Airforce radio frequency is almost as effective as the Tundra Telegraph. One can learn plenty about the best landing areas, flight conditions, etc. simply by paying attention to what the other pilots are reporting to each other.

The chore of preheating was complete, but ski planes don't fly without lots of blue gas on board. I taxied over to the fuel pumps and climbed up on top of the left wing to top her off. Just as I started to pump fuel, a four engine DC6 landed and taxied immediately behind me on the ramp. The pilot of the monster aircraft gestured at me in a menacing manner to move that gnat of an airplane out of his way. He apparently wanted to off load his giant aircraft, which contained enough cargo to feed a village. It was 25 below zero. I figured I would be sitting on the wing for a bit, so I was well covered from head to toe.

I took off my oversized mitten to gesture to the ramp agent that I would move it along as snappy as humanly possible. He gestured, "A-OK" and I reached for the fuel handle with my bare hand. I had neglected to put my mitten on my naked hand. In an effort to speed the process of fueling the plane, I squeezed the handle wide open. As the super-cooled aviation fuel flowed through the aluminum pump handle I felt a burning sensation in my right hand. It felt as though I had grabbed a hand full of red-hot coals. Sure enough, I looked at my hand to find that in that instant my right thumb was beet red. In a New York second I had suffered from frostbite burn as a native later referred to it. Welcome to winter in Alaska. Live and learn, City Boy. Harry told me, "That's going to blister," and it did.

We climbed into the ski plane and departed Unalakleet for Eagle Island in a clear sky and very light winds. As we passed over the hills just southeast of Unalakleet, it got a little bumpy, but not too bad. It was only a 'one bag day' for Harry. The measure of the severity of the turbulence is calculated as follows: light turbulence, one bag; moderate turbulence, two bags; severe turbulence, a small trash bag. Harry would make a great super model. I learned that it is truly a waste of money to buy Harry breakfast in the morning.

We circled Eagle Island a few times and I spied a place to land on the Yukon River. As advertised, it looked like a no-brainer. Even a city boy could land on the Yukon River. The snow appeared very smooth and inviting. The landing area was marked with spruce boughs. I was ready for my first official ski landing without an instructor in the right seat.

I could go on with my bush pilot analysis of the landing area, but in truth there was another telling sign that the landing area was acceptable. Perhaps it was the fact that six other planes and a million-dollar helicopter were sitting immediately in front of the checkpoint at Eagle Island.

We made a long, calculated, flat approach to land on the ski way. I needed a perfect landing. Those six airplanes did not arrive at the checkpoint empty and a large number of tourists were standing adjacent to the landing area, scorecards in hand, ready to judge the gracefulness of my approach and touchdown. It all came together. I greased the ski plane onto the snow-covered Yukon River. The Russian judge gave me a 9.5, but my buddy Harry rated the landing at a perfect 10 and said, "Great first snow landing, bro." I resorted to a quote from Ugashik Bob's book of wisdom, "Well, that's one in a row."

It had become Harry's goal to get face-to-face with newly-famed musher, Lance Mackey. Mackey had won the 1000-mile Yukon Quest International Sled Dog Race for the third time just two weeks ago, and we were curious to find out how many of his dogs from the Quest were running the Iditarod. The local mushers regard the Yukon Quest as the more difficult of the two races. One musher chided the

Iditarod participants by referring to the Iditarod as "a fun little camping trip." It was, and is, hard to believe that Mackey was competing strongly in the Iditarod, after having spent his energy coming off the Quest victory. We were anxious to see his dogs, find out if Mackey was using the same lead dog, and determine whether the dogs appeared fatigued. You don't fly half way across the world to get your information from Megan Baldino. We wanted the inside scoop.

As we trudged through the deep snowy trail to the checkpoint, Harry beamed at the news that Megan Baldino, I JOKE, Lance Mackey had just arrived the checkpoint. Unlike other checkpoints, Eagle Island is a man-made checkpoint, not a village. The checkpoint consisted of a half-made igloo, several tents and stacks of dog food and straw.

As we approached the ravine/gully in which the checkpoint had been situated, we saw Mackey booting his dogs, preparing to leave. Harry approached Mackey in an obviously excited state. Mackey looked up, recognized Harry's elevated enthusiasm, and responded with an appreciative handshake for Harry. Mackey was, no doubt, exhausted. You had to love Mackey's willingness to greet a fan in such a fashion given the energy he had expended just getting to Eagle Island. I thought, "What a sportsman, what a gentleman."

Mackey continued to protect the dog's feet and a TV cameraman from the Outdoor Network pushed the limits of Mackey's patience by shoving a camera square in his face. Mackey was unfazed by the intrusion; he seemed to welcome it. As the crowd around Mackey grew I tested the waters by asking Mackey, "how he was feeling" and asked how many of the fifteen dogs on the team had run the Yukon Quest. Mackey responded with a polite, but cocky, smile, "Thirteen."

There was a collective gasp from the group of tourists that had gathered around Mackey and surrounded his team. I inquired further, "Are they showing any signs of fatigue?" Mackey hesitated to answer the question, again gesturing in an energetic fashion and with a confident tone in his voice, "We did not even get challenged in the last half of the Quest. That race turned out to be a training run

- these dogs are ready to go. Did you see … well … I won't mention any names," Mackey continued, "The other sled dogs as they came in here? They could not wait to lie down? My team would not lie down, they wanted to go right on through, they were playing with each other, I had to wait a few minutes to make sure they would lie down and quit playing with each other."

The cameraman from Outdoor TV cozied up next to me and whispered, "Keep asking him questions, you're doing great." Hmmm, a new career opportunity for me! I asked Mackey if he had a rival on the trail. Mackey responded with a smile, "Yes, EVERYONE." Laughing, he continued, "I am a loner, I have a reputation out here. All the guys ahead of me are looking over their shoulders. Heck, I am only in my 30's; they are all pushing 50 and beyond, they have to be nervous about me."

If the world was not certain to this point in time, it was unmistakably clear that this relatively young man has an abundance of self-confidence. His aggressive manner and attitude bordered on obnoxious, but in balance with his kind demeanor Iditarod fans seemed to walk away with a sense of respect and high regard for his determination. Mackey had command of his team and his audience. Even Harry made the comment to the effect that "Mackey is a manly man."

Harry, SealSkin Phil and I would later debate whether Mackey was over six feet tall. I was of the opinion that Mackey, at best, was of average height. SealSkin Phil, on the other hand, opined that Mackey was over six feet tall, to which I replied, "He just looked tall in stature because he is kicking everyone's butt in the race." He's not a big man, and it pays to be small in dog mushing.

Remember the discussion I had earlier in this journal about carrying a lame dog ninety miles up the Yukon River? Imagine the disadvantage of carrying the added weight of an oversized musher. Mackey's size did not decrease as the discussion and debate continued. When we were visiting with Mackey at the Eagle Island checkpoint, I took off my oversized mitten to take a picture of Mackey and his team. I noticed my blister was getting worse and my hands began to ache from the cold. Harry made moment of the fact that the entire time Mackey was replacing the dog booties he did so without

the benefit of gloves or mittens. Mackey is tough, to be sure. No doubt.

I was not quite ready to relinquish control of the microphone yet, real or imagined, and I asked Mackey if he had a "specific command to direct his team to pass another team while on the trail?" Mackey replied that the rules require that the team being passed give up the trail if they are approached by another team. However, at some point in the race, around White Mountain, just short of Nome, the leader does not have to give up the trail and the passing team must forge their own route around the leader. Nevertheless, Mackey said, "we train our dogs well. If we see another team on the trail, we are to give chase and pass. Besides, the dogs know that I don't like to follow."

With that comment Mackey reached down, removed the snow anchor from the frozen ground and commanded his leaders to advance up the trail. Mackey and his team were headed to Kaltag.

As we walked back to the ski plane I reached into my pocket for a sip of water. You must know that news anchormen work up quite a thirst. As I grabbed the Propel from my pocket I was surprised by the fact that the bottle of water was frozen solid. It drove home the point of what all the mushers and their dogs would continue to endure over the following six days.

I mention 'six days remaining' because the first team to reach Nome typically expends between nine and ten days en route. It takes the final or last team to Nome somewhere short of twenty days to end their journey under the Burled Arch in Nome. The last musher is awarded the "Red Lantern Award" presumably for enduring the abuse on the trail for longer than any other soul.

I was told, unconfirmed rumor of course, that everyone who finishes the race gets a refund of his or her $1049 entry fee. As the story goes, that number "1049" is no accident and has historical significance. The '1000' comes from the fact that the distance covered over the course of the race is roughly 1000 miles. Moreover, Alaska is the 49th State. Hence, the '49.' Using either new or old math, the tally comes to 1049.

When we returned to Unalakleet, we bumped into a couple of pilots from the Iditarod Airforce

("IA"). The IA consists of a group of thirty-two volunteer pilots. The pilots use their personal airplanes to transport over 537 dropped and scratched dogs back to Anchorage. They move over 74000 pounds of dog food, 562 bales of straw and 23200 lathes that mark the Iditarod trail, and countless carpenters, athletes, race judges and volunteers to and from the checkpoints. Would that I could someday serve in the IA, some fun, plenty of responsibility.

One of the IA pilots had a different appearing preheater and I inquired about his 'homemade' heater. He explained and then asked me what we were using to preheat the ski plane each morning. After I told him it's the Northern Companion I mentioned that it burns any type of fuel you put in it and would be great in the event of an unscheduled stop ("Or crash," he says with a whisper). The IA pilot retorted, "Be careful - although the heater will make plenty of heat with camping fuel, etc., you can't boil water at 20 below zero using aviation fuel as your fuel source." Scary, but better I learn that little tidbit of information from him.

We got into a discussion about pilot ratings, etc. He said, "Yes, I am an IFR rated pilot" [laughing]. The term "IFR" means the pilot is qualified to fly under Instrument Flight Rules. Hence, IFR. He continued "In Alaska, I - F - R - means 'I Follow Rivers.' Ha ha. Truly, following major bodies of water, frozen or otherwise, is the safest means to navigate around this neck of the woods. If you get lost up here, find a major body of water, follow it and you will end up in a village eventually.

Today is Sunday, March 11, 2007. The teams are heading towards us as we sit on the ground in Unalakleet. We are not planning on flying today. Rather, we will wait here for the mushers. Naturally, today would have to be a perfect day to fly. Clear sky, calm winds. It is only windy and snowy on the days you really want to fly. In fact, the more you want to fly, the worse the weather will get, it seems. The mushers will make a stop in the village of Shaktoolik, and then push their teams across the sea ice on the Norton Sound towards Nome.

One of the more famous tales I have heard on this trip came from a native woman from the village of Shaktoolik. As the story goes, Libby Riddles and her boyfriend trained their dogs in Nome, Alaska. On a Sunday night in 1985, she mushed thirteen dogs out of Shaktoolik and into the teeth of a blizzard that pinned every other racer to the village. The other mushers warned Libby that if she made the run across the Norton Sound she was sure to die in the blizzard. Libby called home to Nome and discussed the situation with her partner, Joe Gurney. Gurney told Libby to point the team towards home; they would find their way across the ice-laden Norton Sound. The daring move gave Riddles a

lead that couldn't be overcome, and she reached Nome three days later as the first woman ever to win the Iditarod.

In anticipation of our departure to Nome over the coming days, I have been studying the terrain surrounding Unalakleet and Nome. Unlike the beginning of the trip, the terrain surrounding this part of Alaska is relatively flat. The highest point along our flight route to Nome is only 2100 feet. Compare that elevation to the Rainy Pass and the Aleutian Range. The Aleutian Range covers a line of mountains that rise to 20,000 feet, with McKinley (aka Denali) at the peak at 20,350 feet. This is the highest point in North America. The native people call it the "Great One" or Denali. The snowfields along the range are considered a permanent part of the landscape and cover fifty percent of the mountain.

The landscape we traveled over during the early days of the trip was covered with glaciers. It seems like there were too many to count. The Nome area is wanting for glaciers. Of all the pictures we took in the first half the trip, we were only able to get close to the Matanuska Glacier in the Palmer area where we landed for "cheap gas" (with Papa Amish). The Matanuska Glacier is twenty-seven miles long, four miles wide, and one-thousand feet thick. Although the glaciers here in Alaska advance or move forward an average of two feet per day, the increased global temperatures are causing a loss of twenty-five to thirty feet of melting ice each year. In any event, I am looking forward to not having to battle the high terrain while navigating towards Nome. The temperatures at the higher altitudes could become a problem for the ski plane. The low-lying mountains, hills really, will allow us to stay in the minus 15 to minus 20-degree range, which has not been a problem for the ski plane.

SealSkin Phil just got a call from his nephew. Apparently, Phil's nephew was out on the trail and spotted the first musher coming into Unalakleet. It looks to be Jeff King.

We just returned from the Iditarod checkpoint and, as rumored, Jeff King is the first musher into the village. King, like Martin Buser, is a four-time winner of the Iditarod. As I watched King unpack his sled and prepare to care for the dogs, he was slow and methodical in changing booties, heating and

feeding, making repairs to his sled, etc. There was no apparent sense of urgency for this seasoned musher.

The second musher into Unalakleet was team Mackey. When Mackey arrived, King's demeanor changed significantly. King watched Mackey at the first opportunity and continuously watched the dogs from 1000 yards out as they tracked into the checkpoint. The remainder of the crowd, including King, locked onto Mackey. I was more fascinated by King's response and I was riveted by the fact that the seasoned King was visibly shaken by Mackey's proximity to his team. Apparently, King thought the always-pesky team Mackey would have burned out by now.

It was at the point of Mackey's arrival that King's attitude changed. For the first time in the race I had witnessed the more experienced mushers reacting to young Mackey. King picked up the pace noticeably.

The instant the sled came to a halt, Mackey was swift in getting busy preparing his team. His dog team seemed to be in tune with his energy level and sensed Mackey's quest to move quickly through Unalakleet and up the trail. None of the dogs laid down and the two lead dogs barked until it was obvious that Mackey intended to rest the team. Mackey has never won an Iditarod, although he has been a top-ten finisher.

The third team into Unalakleet was Martin Buser. Buser is the musher that I mentioned has run the race twenty-four times. Both Buser and his team appeared to be fatigued, as they came to rest here. But how can you count a musher with Buser's experience out of the race at any point? He can run the trail blindfolded or, at least as it seems right now, in his sleep.

The fourth musher into Unalakleet was Paul Gephart. He trailed the leader by about an hour. I was so preoccupied with watching Jeff King's face as Mackey arrived, that I hardly had a chance to see Gephart and his team of dogs come into the village.

When Gephart arrived he immediately laid down straw for the dogs. His lead dog refused to lie down and he said, "Oh, this is not going to work." He expeditiously took the dog off the lead and placed him at the back of the pack near the wheel dogs, which is just in front of the sled. I was not certain whether this was a permanent change or just a move to psyche the leader out.

When an Iditarod vet approached Gephart, he said he intended to drop at least one dog from the team in Unalakleet. I figured he was having problems with his leader, which could be a major blow to team Gephart.

I remained astonished about how the people in the village are permitted to interact with the mushers and the dogs. There are no ropes or anything stopping the observers from walking up to the mushers. On more than one occasion a musher has had to push his way through the crowd to feed and tend to his team.

The children in the village can, and do, pet the dogs. Here in Unalakleet, the village elders used a tractor to stack a four-foot berm of snow creating four lanes for the dog teams to enter as they approached the village on the river. The berms are basically boulders of snow and the kids in the village climb on the berms just above the dogs. As the kids climb on the snow banks, the boulders of snow drop off onto the dogs. In sum, no one is restricting the activities of the kids. There is the obvious potential that a tourist or kid from the village could injure himself or a sled dog. In Alaska, the interaction between the fans and the mushers is a fact of life. Perhaps it is indicative of a way of life. Representative really. Refreshing, yet frightening.

I guess if the race organizers created barriers for the race in the same fashion that we isolate the athletes from the fans 'down in America' the obstacles would change the complexion of the race and it would not have the same feel that it does now. The level of excitement I have experienced here in the village is unlike anything I have experienced as a fan at a major sporting event. The interaction that takes place is complex. It exists between mushers, officials, fans, dogs - all at the same time. I came to watch dogs and mushers, but everyone seems to get in the act. It is fascinating.

With regard to the musher-dog interaction, one story that is often repeated is the story of a mutiny by Deedee Jonrowe's dog team. I am told that in 1999 the temperatures on the Yukon River got down to 75-below, wind chill, hammering the frozen Yukon River. Jonrowe saw her 1999 Iditarod dream come to an abrupt and unexpected end when she scratched from the race for the first time in her career. This year would be her second early departure from the race.

A revolt by her twelve-dog team caught the popular Willow musher as much off-guard as it did officials of the Iditarod Trail Sled Dog Race and the legion of fans that have been following the perennial front-runner's progress. There was no advance warning for Jonrowe. Jonrowe's team had performed

flawlessly and looked strong in checkpoints going north.

In the predawn darkness, a once steadily trot-
ting dog team began to balk, alternating between stopping and starting. But her main leader decided he didn't want to continue into the
wind and minus 30-degree cold. He would stop
and go, stop and go, the other leader adopted
the same behavior and the entire team followed
suit, ending the race for Jonrowe.

As we track the teams to Nome, it is worth
noting that Nome is famous for more than just the finish line of the Iditarod (Front Street). The dis-
covery of gold in Nome, at Anvil and Snow Creeks, resulted in Alaska's greatest gold rush - in terms
of yield and the number of people involved. An estimated 40,000 people were attracted to an area
previously inhabited by only a handful of settlers. These goldseekers mined more than $60 million of
gold by 1911 from area creeks and beaches.

Nome is still popular as a destination for goldminers. In the summer months, miners still come to
West Beach and pan for gold. There is rumored to be a great place to pan for gold just north of the
airport. If my career in news casting does not pan out, maybe I can dredge up some gold in Nome.
Stay tuned.

We returned to the checkpoint [still in Unalakleet] this evening to see the mushers off to Shaktoolik.
All the members of the media surrounded Mackey and his team. Mackey is as much the entertainer as
he is the dog musher. He told the collected crowd that he wanted to win this race more than the other
three mushers currently resting in Unalakleet. Besides, he exclaimed, "My truck broke down on my
way to the race, so I need that new truck sitting in Nome." Mackey, of course, was referring to the
oversized Dodge truck awarded to the winner of the Iditarod.

Mackey continued to complete his chores as he entertained the local villagers and tourists alike. One
of the items on the to-do list for mushers is to change the runners on the dog sled. The runners are
located on the bottom of the sled rails and can be removed or swapped out depending on the snow or
ice conditions. If the snow is hard and fast, the musher uses a white rail. If the snow is wet and sloppy,

the musher uses a red rail, and so forth.

As Mackey labored to change his rails, I meandered over to Paul Gephart's team. I overheard Gephart tell a reporter that he had waited eleven years to win the Iditarod and he was anxious to be the first musher out of Unalakleet. Since the mushing world was having a love affair with Mackey, it should come as no surprise that I found myself standing alone with Gephart. I was enamored with his mumbling and enjoyed the one-on-one time with the musher. Gephart glanced over at Mackey and the crowd of fans, but not quite with the energy that King exhibited. Gephart turned to me and mumbled, "Changing those rails is not going to make a bit of difference - the sand and gravel between here and Shaktoolik will rip the rails to shreds."

I noticed that Gephart was down to ten dogs, compared to Mackey's fourteen dogs on the line and King's team of thirteen. I asked him if the reduced numbers in his team of dogs would change anything for him over the next several hundred miles? He said, "Yes, less work," referring to the reduced chores he would have to perform with fewer dogs.

I had to question the logic. Was he just saying that to me because he was upset at being down to a team of ten dogs? I mean, common sense would dictate that having fourteen dogs sharing the load is better than ten? Let's face it, having four additional dogs sharing the pulling responsibility reduces the workload, conserves energy and makes for more pulling power when going uphill. Why do you think they put all them horses in the new Ford Mustang? I mean eight cylinders are better than six, but Gephart would argue that eight cylinders require more gas. I guess we will have to wait for the answer to that riddle in Nome.

I also formed an opinion about the dog food. At each stop the mushers would boil water and pour it over varying types of food, including: salmon, herring, tripe (cow guts), pork, moose meat, seal oil, store bought dog food, etc. Many of the mushers gave the dogs frozen fish. It seems odd to me that the dogs would be given ANYTHING frozen. The outside air temperatures were brutally cold, and the dogs seemingly were burning energy simply to maintain their core temperature. It seemed like a

needless waste of the dog's energy to give them frozen food, which would require that the dog's body heat be used to heat the fish through the digestive process. Maybe I am missing something here, but it seems prudent to heat the food for the dogs, as was being done, to reduce the burden on their weary bodies. Just an observation.

Monday, March 12, 2007. By now, it is apparent that Harry, SealSkin Phil and I are rooting for Mackey. We are not alone. The villagers can't hide their enthusiasm for Mackey, and the press loves him too. I inquired of Scotty, a cameraman for Channel 2 News, "You have to believe that a personality like Mackey is good for the Iditarod - a great media figure, yes?" Scotty agreed, "Just look around us. There are four mushers here, two of those mushers have run the Iditarod four times, Paul (Gephart) consistently places in the top ten, and we are all huddled around Lance Mackey."

Oddly, the stoical Gephart agrees with Scotty, although not publicly. I mentioned earlier that I was hovering around Gephart while the rest of the world fawned over Mackey. That was the point at which Gephart mumbled that changing the runners would not make a difference. Gephart is smaller in stature physically than Mackey. The two mushers also have strikingly different personalities. Gephart mumbles and grumbles his way through the crowd and checkpoint, moving slowly but methodically through the crowd while caring for the dogs.

Mackey, on the other hand, moves through the crowd like the court jester, with his dogs playing the part of the gaily colored mascots. Mackey is having fun. When Mackey is not laughing with the fans and reporters, he is playing the part of a young boy with a stick and a picket fence versus an obnoxious dog on the other side of the fence. Mackey runs up and down the fence, stick in hand, railing the stick against the fence in an attempt to drive the barking dog, still on the opposite side of the fence, crazy.

Mackey would run up and down the fence all day, but who has time to toy with a dog when he has a race to run!

Oh yes, we were discussing Gephart's comment about Mackey. While I was playing a fly on the wall, a race official took a knee next to Gephart and, although I did not hear the official's comment, I heard Gephart say, "Mackey is good for the race, no matter who gets to Nome first." It is obvious that Mackey's youth and energy level are having a psychological impact on the older mushers. They seem to be looking over their collective shoulders in disbelief. Mackey and thirteen of the dogs dragging him towards Nome just finished, and handily won, the Yukon Quest. In years past when the Quest champ attempted to compete in the Iditarod, he and his team burned out early in the second race. Mackey is not only going away, he seems to be in the face of the more seasoned mushers.

Since this is the first time I have observed the race, I would be surprised if the two former champs don't have a multitude of tricks in their sleds. While they appear to be thinking that the race appears to be Mackey's to lose, there is an equal chance that they are thinking, "Just keep talking, punk, I will laugh all the way to the Dodge dealership." I am the rookie. Only time will tell.

Our arrival into Nome was somewhat uneventful. The weather was picture perfect with a blue sky and only ten knots of wind out of the north, where else? We followed a Cessna 185 to the 'big' airport and he elected to land downwind on the south runway, with the wind. I did not understand why he elected to land with the wind, except maybe he figured that he would be closer to a good parking spot. Not to be outdone, I followed the Cessna the wrong direction down the runway and landed with the wind on the hard-surfaced runway.

The Cessna taxied over to the public ramp. We had our secret weapon in the back seat, SealSkin Phil, so we taxied over to a private hangar operated by ------ Airways. Phil's brother, Chuck, is a plumbing contractor in this part of Alaska. Chuck, apparently well liked and well known, has friends and vehicles at every airport in this part of the state. As a result, we were able to taxi the plane up to a private parking spot. This spot had the added benefit of access to 120-watt power outlet. It was a small victory to take a 100-foot power cord out of the back of the ski plane and plug the electric heater on the belly of the oil pan into a power outlet.

I was smiling because the electric heater on the oil pan is in lieu of the painful process of preheating the plane with the portable gas stove, The Northern Companion. The gas stove takes two hours to

preheat the plane, while the electric oil pan allows us to walk up, climb into the ski plane and go flying.

Aside from the welcome mat for Phil's brother, we also draw a crowd because SealSkin Phil has one of the most unique sealskin jackets in all of Alaska. I know this because every native we passed on the trail wanted to touch, discuss and trade for that jacket.

We loaded our gear into the back of the fully loaded plumbing service vehicle. All was going well in Nome until we hooked up with our host in Nome, one George the Contractor. Around a month short of our arrival in Nome, SealSkin Phil had arranged for accommodations with George the Contractor. George had promised Phil that we could stay at his recently remodeled apartment building, which allegedly is one-hundred yards from the finish line of the Iditarod.

As we pulled the plumber's van up to George's Tyvek Manor we were struck by the fact that the building was still encased in Tyvek - (the plastic used by contractors to protect a building from the weather during a remodel) and was recently about to be remodeled. Actually, the Tyvek Manor was more accurately in the tearing-down stages of the remodel than in the rebuilding phase. There were partially covered walls, exposed wires, tools scattered everywhere, dust, dirt, mildew covering old appliances and furniture partially covered and being stored, etc. etc. etc.

As the three of us made our way up the stairs behind George, he apologized in earnest for slightly exaggerating the status of the remodel. As we reached the third floor, George forced the door open and to the surprise of the four of us, and the two of them, we were not alone in the Tyvek Manor. Apparently, the current occupants had been requested "to get out over 24 hours ago." George exclaimed to his holdover tenants "I already told you to get out, is that going to be a problem?" The tenant had

a striking resemblance to Charles Manson. We aptly nicknamed him, Dave the Serial Killer. He replied in a menacing tone, "I think it is going to be a BIG PROBLEM."

Needless to say, we made it our mission to find another warm place to put our heads on a pillow that night. We went to the local Italian restaurant for dinner and the Chinese owner was kind enough to let us use his telephone to call every hotel and B&B in Nome. There simply were no rooms available. Harry suggested we head back to the plane, get the tent and survival gear and sleep on the beach. Uh . . . no thanks.

SealSkin Phil mentioned that he had yet another "friend", Jack the Miner who might have a place for us to stay for the night. Jack the Miner resided at a locale the Nomers call West Beach. To refresh your recollection, West Beach is famous as a site for gold mining. This is the area that, in 1900, had a population explosion that went from a few hundred to 40,000 people over night. The legend is told: Wyatt Earp and 39,999 of his closest friends came to Nome in 1900 to strike it rich. If you ever see a picture of Nome during the gold rush, you will see literally thousands of tents. Those tents are sitting on and around West Beach.

Eight to ten squatter's cabins have replaced those tents. The cabins are made from pressed wood, plywood, old pallets, and driftwood. Basically, the cabins are made of any material that washes up on the beach or can be salvaged from the local dump. In order to heat these palaces, most of the squatters have cut metal 55-gallon drums in half and use them as wood burning stoves.

As we approached Jack the Miner's place, I noted that Jack is one of the wealthier miners on West Beach, given the two cars "parked" in his front yard. It may be a bit of a stretch to say parked, since the cars were buried under four feet of snow and apparently had not moved since the turn of the century.

Jack welcomed us to his place, asked if we brought him any "whissssskkeee" and promptly fell on his posterior. It would be a monumental overstatement to say that Jack the Miner was slightly intoxicated. As Jack gathered himself, he found the handle to the front door and attempted to pull the door open several times, only to be reminded by us newcomers that the door appeared to be a slider.

As the door slid open, smoke rushed out of the cabin and I asked Jack if the chimney from his wood stove was obstructed. Jack replied, "Nah, we haven't had the wood stove going all week." I suspected that Jack and his friends had a problem with more than just alcohol!

As we all settled in the cabin, Harry sat in the study with SealSkin Phil, Jack sat in the kitchen with his new squaw April, and I sat in the kitchen. Okay, I admit it we basically sat in a small circle in this multipurpose one room cabin. There appeared to be more pot and alcohol in that twenty-square-foot area than Time Square on New Year's Eve.

Jack tried to pass me April's peace pipe, but Harry mentioned the fact that the "fellas from the California State Bar frown upon that sort of thing." April, chiming in on cue said, "Oh, you're a lawyer...I have a problem." Naturally I was surprised, given April's current living conditions, that she had a problem.

I replied, "Yes, April, I am a lawyer, but lawyers don't work for free. I have a problem as well. If you solve my problem, I will be glad to solve your problem. Can I go first?" April gave me the drunken stare and said, "Uh, yup."

I informed April that the boys and I needed a warm, clean and serial-killer-free place to stay. Since April was a local girl, she had to know someone with such accommodations.

April said, "No problem, my apartment is about one-hundred feet from the finish line. I am shacking up with Jack. You guys can crash at my place." I mentioned that lawyers normally get their fee up front, so I poured them into the back of the plumber's van and we were off to April's apartment. April sat in the front seat to give me directions and so that I could answer a series of legal questions.

Although I had my lawyer's cap ready for April, she passed out on the trip over. Not to worry though, Jack knew the way to April's place and after an extended tour of Nome, we happened onto April's place. As promised, it was clean, warm and had a lock on the door to keep us safe from Dave the Serial Killer. Better yet, you literally could throw a snowball and hit the finish line of the Iditarod.

Although Nome is probably a sleepy little village for 360 days of the year, the buzz around the finish line of the race gave me the feeling that the Gold Rush was not so long ago. It felt like we were visiting a place in time, not just a place.

Prior to our arrival in Nome, SealSkin Phil had made it clear to Harry and I that SealSkin's goal was to visit every bar in Nome wearing, of course, his seal skin coat, and to consume the equivalent of a

55-gallon drum of beer. So off we went to fulfill his dream. After two beers, I get sleepy and everyone around me starts to sound like my high school chemistry teacher, so I packed it in early.

On Tuesday, March 13, we awoke to the sound of snow machines in front of April's apartment. Phil's brother, Chuck the Plumber, had arrived in Nome with four or five other snow-machiners. The gang had seen the plumber's van out front and figured that SealSkin Phil could not be far from the van. It was at that point in time that I learned it was Chuck and his sidekicks that 'break trail' for the Iditarod mushers. Chuck and the gang had started the race in Willow and traveled the entire 1000+ miles to Nome placing trail markers along the Iditarod trail for mushers and the teams to follow.

Chuck's son, JR, said that they had come from the White Mountain Checkpoint, which is about seventy miles from Nome. It is at the White Mountain Checkpoint that the mushers and their teams must take their mandatory eight-hour rest before the final push to Safety, and then Nome. The trailbreakers had an annual tradition of stopping in White Mountain for a celebratory King Crab Dinner, compliments of Chuck the Plumber. Before they could boil the pot of water a soon to be famous musher and a team of nine dogs slid into White Mountain, surprising the villagers, trailbreakers and fans alike.

By all accounts, Mackey was on a record pace, leaving Gephart two hours in his snowdust. When JR asked Mackey how he was feeling, Mackey replied, "Great, but my fingers are killing me." Mackey proceeded to remove the glove from his right hand. JR said Mackey's "Ring and middle finger were black from the middle knuckle to the tip." Can you imagine? Mackey will likely lose a part of those fingers as his sacrifice for becoming the first musher to win the Quest and Iditarod in the same year.

Although I knew little about Mackey before the Yukon Quest, as a precursor to this Iditarod adventure, I paid close attention to the Quest this year and have been intrigued since watching him win the Quest. The Iditarod win also marks the sixth year Lance Mackey has competed in the race. His father Dick and brother Rick won the Iditarod on their sixth try as well.

All three Mackeys were wearing bib number 13 when they pulled into Nome first. That is quite a legacy, three Iditarod champions from the same family.

When the race started, it was my impression that Mackey was starting from nowhere. When I heard the story about his truck breaking down on the way to the race, I assumed he and his family were in survival mode as their sacrifice for Mackey's goal of winning the major races. But clearly, Mackey had the benefit of a kennel full of fantastic, trailblazing dogs. During the stop at the Eagle Island checkpoint, I had asked Mackey how many of the dogs in his team were related by blood. Mackey replied, pointing at the lead dog first, "Father, son, sister, sister, brother, daughter", etc. The entire team stemmed from the lead dog, a good sized, handsome male. Like racehorses out of the Kentucky Derby, these dogs had been bred for generations to bring a sled to Nome. The Mackey family had the benefit of a few generations of breeding and the ability to select the cream of the crop from within the kennel.

Prior to leaving America for my trip to Alaska, I had read a story about a city slicker or two that had the dream to win the Iditarod. As I understand it, there are a number of former Iditarod contenders who will rent you a team. Now that sounds like the hobby of the idle rich! The former racer will train the race tourist for two years, and effectively, set the race tourist up for the big race. I thought this was an interesting proposition.

As an 'on the ground' or 'in the village observer' of the Iditarod, I realized that renting a team would be, as Nomers say, "Fools gold." There can be no replacement for experience as a musher, or for years of creative or effective breeding.

During the two years of impersonating an Iditarod musher, how could a race tourist learn all that is learned over a lifetime of mushing? How can you compete with a musher, like Mackey, whose father and brother were champions? How much had Mackey learned through osmosis from overhearing his father talking to other mushers, vets and competitors; tying and untying dogs, feeding and not feeding dogs? How much had flowed effortlessly through young Lance Mackey's head without the typical obstacles that naturally exist between father and son?

Lest we forget Mark Twain's quote: "When I was a boy of twelve my father was so stupid I could hardly stand to be around him. When I turned eighteen, I was surprised at how much the old man had learned in a few short years." Mackey would have none of that. Yes, he likely had the years, like all of us, in which he and the 'old man' did not see eye-to-eye. But in the end, that did not inhibit or limit what he would inherit as a musher. What's in the cat is in the kitten! Mackey had musher in his blood whether he knew it, wanted it or not!

Rent a team? Hogwash. Just like renting a guide to help you climb Everest, this race can kill the ill prepared. Chap, you should read the book "Into Thin Air" at some point as an example of how taking a shortcut, and renting your way into the wilderness, can kill you. You know the routine, "If the cheese is free, it is in a trap."

Over the course of the race, as we stopped in each village and studied the team, I asked myself, "How would a rent-a-team musher, a race tourist, really know what to do?" Besides, isn't renting a team kind of like picking up a lost golf ball while it is still rolling? Not exactly fair play given the sacrifice made by the other mushers.

But how would you know when to feed the dogs; what to feed the dogs; when to rest; how to deal with a headwind; do you have one lead dog or two; if you pull your lead dog, does it hurt his or her feelings; do you continue down the trail when you feel good, but the dogs are tired; do you continue down the trail when the dogs feel good and you feel tired; can you force your dogs to rest, can you afford to take a cat-nap on a dog sled; does a male or female dog make the best lead dog; can you have two lead dogs, one being female and one being a male lead dog, at the same time; hot food or cold food; do you feed pork or fish first; is dried food harder to digest in the middle of a race; do you need booties in soft snow; if you put the wrong sized bootie on a given dog, will he or she be upset and not perform well; do the dogs run because they love the musher, the trail, the competition, the camaraderie, what; do you pass another dog team if the wind is in your face just because you taught your team not to follow; does the musher know and understand the weather conditions two days hence so he/she can decide to push on in good weather today and rest during the poor weather at some point in the future; does the team have better performance on flat ground or on hilly terrain; can the dogs make the sprint in the last leg, Safety to Nome; is there a point in the race that it is actually to the teams advantage to have fewer dogs; is it better to heat the food with propane or 'heet'; gloves or mittens; better to sit or stand; military bunny boots or Cabela Arctic boots; wood or aluminum sled; big dogs in the lead or, slender, faster dogs; necklines or harnesses for the dogs; blankets to keep the dogs warm during stops or let them lay in straw only; leave a village with a minor injury or drop the dog immediately; drop a female 'in season' or risk distracting the male dogs; reduce the amount of food/supplies in your sled mid-race, or burden the team with weight to ensure the welfare of the dogs and musher; run with frozen hands, even if they have to be amputated after the race; leave the booties off the dogs on the last leg because they run better without booties and you are close to the finish; change lead dogs because it creates a competitive atmosphere within the team or risk the change in lead dogs and break the spirit of the superior lead dog; let a one-year-old dog run the race; return to a checkpoint in bad weather or keep forward progress and hunker down; let the other mushers think you're tired; let the other mushers think you're fresh; stop every two hours to give the dogs treats or snacks; give the lead dogs fish as their treat and the swing dogs pork; snacking more frequently as the race progresses; cooked or raw food; moose meat or cow meat; what to do if a dog refuses to eat; does the musher wear a helmet or a beaver hat AND THE MILLIONS OF OTHER QUESTIONS, the answers to which are better learned over a generation and not during a rent-a-team crash course.

As my former baseball coach, John the Man from 'Buuooston' used to say, "D'eir ain't no sani claus boyz ...I didn't just fall out of a tree when I was eighteen yeeaars old and learn how to hit a baseball, boyz, it tuuuk wuurk." There is no free lunch in baseball, on the trail or in life.

As the champions approached the finish line, we headed for race headquarters at the local banquet hall in Nome. The building is around 40 yards long and 20 yards wide, filled with souvenirs for sale, race boards, phones, computers, etc. It is here that the increasing number of fans attempt to learn the fate of their favorite mushing team.

As we followed the teams to Nome, there were times on the trail that we had the mushers and teams all to ourselves. It was like a local fishing hole. It was "ours," we owned it, save for the occasional interloper we tolerated for short intervals. That was lost now. The world had discovered our secret and they were all waiting in Nome. In an odd way, the race has taken on a new personality. It had been transformed from a quaint event to a major sporting event. Where McGrath held the potential that Martin Buser would say, "Hold this sled anchor," Nome had a new directive "Behind the fence, please, sir." When I hear the word "sir" I feel compelled to look around for my father.

Not to worry, the gift of the early days of the Iditarod Race, our days and hours in the villages, are forever embedded in my mind. Although I had intended this Journal to be my gift to you, the process of sitting down to hand write you this Journal has memorialized the event for all of us.

It is clear now that Mackey will be the next Iditarod champion. He is rumored to be so far ahead of the pack, that he is stopping along the trail outside of Nome to sign autographs, shaking hands, etc. Since we are standing in a large crowd behind the barrier on Front Street, in Nome, we really have no clue what is happening outside of our field of view.

As Mackey approaches the finish line, the public announcer is broadcasting trivia about past races: "Lance Mackey's father won the Iditarod on his sixth attempt, as did his brother; Mackey's father and brother both won the race wearing lucky number 13; this is Mackey's sixth attempt at an Iditarod win and he is wearing bib 13."

As Mackey came into view down Front Street, the crowd roared and victory-danced under the arch in Nome. It had the feeling of an Olympic Event. Uncharacteristically, I felt overwhelmed momentarily, taken in by the monumental moment. Although I had taken the easy route to Nome, I had a sense of what the musher had endured. For the rest of the world, the Iditarod was a series of still pictures. For Harry and me, it was a motion picture with a storybook ending. It was a privilege to be a part of it.

I don't really understand why people all over America don't get excited about The Last Great Race. Especially this race. I mean, the outcome of this year's race is the equivalent of a Triple Crown in horse racing. I know when I return to America that the race will get a one liner in most newspapers, and the gratuitous comments will flow from liberals mischaracterizing this as a cruel thing to do to the dogs.

Is it a cruel thing to do to racehorses? I guess the racehorse lobbyists have deeper pockets than the average lobbyist from Shaktoolik, Alaska! My distinct impression from watching the dogs, and I had no preconceived notions, was that they were having a wonderful time. Of the countless number of times I witnessed a dog sled come into a village, I did not see a dog that appeared exhausted. In fact, the overwhelming number of dogs appeared anxious to get back on the trail. The dogs, more than the mushers, were having the time of their lives. The dogs will run, to a point, due to their love for their musher, but when the wind starts blowing 40 knots they do what their instincts tell them to do.

As for the accomplishment of the musher, Mackey and his team had accomplished the equivalent of

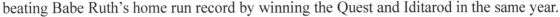

beating Babe Ruth's home run record by winning the Quest and Iditarod in the same year.

You might recall that earlier I had pontificated in Unalakleet about whether Gephart could compete with just nine dogs. Buser, Mackey and King all left Unalakleet with between twelve and fourteen dogs in harness. The answer came two hours later when Team Gephart arrived in Nome with nine dogs on the line. Sadly, the majority of the crowd was all but gone. It was brutally clear to me that dog mushing has but one major champion, and seventy or so people who follow. I don't want to leave you with the impression that all the participants are not treated with respect. That is not the case at all. Each of the racers is celebrated and I think the Red Lantern Award, hanging on the Arch in Nome, is representative of that fact. But the majority of the celebration that night surrounded Mackey. After watching all the teams suffer through the race, I wanted each musher to get the sensation that the world was waiting for them in Nome. I believe that anyone with the fortitude to endure 1100+ miles of unforgiving terrain in subzero temperatures deserves a hero's welcome.

It was late, or as I like to say, "Time to check my eyelids for light holes." Bedtime. As I drifted off into a deep sleep, my calm thoughts were interrupted by the thunder of a drunken Jack the Miner entering the house and stepping squarely on my head. Jack asked me, "Do you have anything to eat around here?" I replied, "Beer, it's not just for breakfast anymore." Try as I might, I could not get back to sleep. It would have been futile, as SealSkin Phil appeared on the scene shortly thereafter appearing very downtrodden and slightly intoxicated. He said that his lucky sealskin coat seemed jinxed, as the local ladies in Nome seemed unimpressed with the magic coat. I told SealSkin Phil he was not giving the native girls the whole story. You need to tell them, "Clubbed, not shot -- that's the ticket with the native chicks!" He was not amused. Am I just not funny, or did SealSkin Phil just have too much to drink? Help me out here?

After the 'night's rest,' Harry and I got up before the sun and headed to the airport. We departed Nome in relatively clear skies, encountered overcast layers which forced us along the shoreline adding another 1/2 hour to our 2+-hour flight to Unalakleet. We refueled with all the efficiency of an Indy 500 Pit Crew and headed for McGrath. Unlike the reverse leg of the trip, we had clear skies and a perfect view of the mighty Yukon River. There would be no picking our way through passes all the way home. The outside air temperature at our cruising altitude was a brisk minus 15 degrees. The plane ran flawlessly.

We arrived in McGrath and again refueled the plane in record time. As we left McGrath, and as I al-

ways do, I called the Kenai Flight Service Station to advise them of our departure from McGrath, our destination, routing and time en route. It is imperative that someone knows where we are and where we are going. If we fail to show up at the appointed time, I trust that a search and rescue will follow. We started our slow and steady climb towards - the maze - Rainy Pass. As we climbed out of 6500 feet the engine seemed to make a light, but noticeable, rumble. I ignored it, for a moment, thinking a change in wind direction and speed could cause the propeller to make such noise. It happened again and I asked Harry, "Are you hearing that too?" Harry said, "I think so."

As we continued our climb to a higher altitude the "rumble" turned into a gnarly miss. The fuselage of the ski plane was now beginning to vibrate a bit with each absent cylinder. The phrase, "Houston, we have a problem." came to mind. Like most pilots with an engine problem, I wanted to get as far away from the ground as possible. So, we climbed higher, making the trees as small as possible and I made the turn back towards McGrath.

I tried to remedy the problem by switching from the left fuel tank to the right fuel tank, thinking we might have water in our fuel tanks and lines. I still got ugly reports from the engine.

Okay, let's try different magnetos. I turned the key to the right mag, left mag, both mags. Still ugly.

Hmmm, maybe we have ice in the carburetor. Although I had been applying 'carb heat' frequently throughout the flight, I tried it again, this time for an extended period. The ski plane continued to run like 'Chitty chitty bang bang.' Not good.

Well, "This isn't good," said the city pilot thinking it would be a long, cold, night in the Alaskan bush. I looked at the outside air temperature, minus 35 degrees. Wow, I had not seen more than minus 30 degrees at any point in the trip. Maybe the ski plane does not like the extreme temperatures. I played with the mixture- in, more fuel; out, less fuel. Nothing was working, and I had pushed and pulled on every knob in the ski plane.

Worse yet, the trees were now getting bigger as we made our undesirable descent. I called the Flight Service Station in Kenai, Alaska to let them know that we were experiencing engine problems and intended to return to McGrath. The representative from the Flight Service Station asked if we needed any assistance. I thought, "Now that's an interesting question coming from someone seated in a heated office 250 miles away. HMMM, yes, please send two qualified aircraft mechanics, and pepperoni and sausage pizza with extra thick crust." What the heck? ASSISTANCE!!

Ultimately, gravity would win the battle with wimpy engine and as we descended out of 6000 feet we had the airport well in sight and a landing assured. Out of an altitude of 3000 feet, we were squarely over the airport. The outside air temperature had increase to minus 15 degrees and the engine noise was not as nasty. Although the engine was running poorly, it was not running as poorly as it had been at the higher altitudes in the colder temperatures.

We crossed over the airport centerline, and I made the turn to downwind with plenty of altitude. I let the Flight Service Station know we had the 'airport made' and cancelled the order for the pepperoni and sausage. I asked Harry if I experimented with the various controls as we circled for a landing, but as I pushed and pulled all the colorful knobs and switches, the engine continued to run at less than full capacity. We landed without incident.

I made several calls in an attempt to find a qualified aircraft maintenance professional. Let's face it, McGrath, Alaska is not a metropolis. I had a local mechanic look at the plane. He swore the plane was getting too much fuel. He made some adjustments, and we were off again for the frozen maze. We initially climbed the ski plane to just 3000 feet, wanting to keep ourselves in the relatively warm temperature, 20 below zero. The engine ran fine, life was good.

About an hour into our second attempt at the Rainy Pass, we arrived at that fateful moment of the flight, which required that we climb to a higher altitude. Although it is possible to travel through the pass at a much lower altitude than I intended to fly, I lacked the 'home-boy' familiarity with the Rainy Pass and I wanted the excess altitude to ensure I did not fly into a blind canyon. And, heaven forbid, should the ski plane turn into a glider, I would need the altitude to find a good place to land and camp.

As we stared into the pass, I felt like a guppy staring into the mouth of Moby Dick. As we climbed out of 3000 feet, to an altitude of 4000 feet, the engine began to cough. "That's not good." Harry knows I follow Mark Twain's motto that, "It is better to be cautious a thousand times than dead once." I did not want to be among the collection of aircraft sitting in the bottom of the Rainy Pass. We turned the noisy end of the plane towards McGrath, called the Kenai Flight Service Station and got a hearty, "Welcome back." The noisy end of the plane stayed noisy for the entire hour it took to get back to McGrath and we landed uneventfully in McGrath.

By now, I had all I could take of the local aviation maintenance professionals in McGrath, so I called my trusted friend, Satellite Sam.

If it wasn't for bad luck I was having no luck at all. But as luck would have it, Satellite Sam was just over the mountains in Anchorage on a special assignment. Sam is always the one to embrace an adventure and, no doubt, wanted to be a friend. He said he would fly to McGrath in the morning to help me out.

I awoke the following morning to temperatures approaching minus 20 degrees and light winds out of the North, of course. I did not relish the idea of dismantling a plane on a cold, snow encrusted tarmac in sub-zero temperatures, but a man has to do what a man has to do. On the other hand, any sissy can fix a plane in an air-conditioned hangar in South Florida, so I accepted the challenge as a notable page in my journal of life.

As I dismantled the ski plane on the icy airport, a kind fella from the Department of Transportation ("DOT") came by to say 'hello.' He had a plane similar to the ski plane and we talked about my options. He took pity on me and said that I should pull the ski plane in front of the maintenance garage by the DOT building so that I could duck in out of the cold from time to time. I thought, "Now that's what I'm talkin' about."

I pushed the plane over to the area immediately in front of the maintenance garage. As I started to remove the cowling from the ski plane, the garage door rolled open and a gentleman from the DOT pushed the world's largest jet-propelled heater out of the garage and immediately in front of the ski plane. God bless the guys from the DOT!

I took all the equipment and covers out of the back of the ski plane and made myself a miniature heated tent. I removed all that I could from the plane to expedite Satellite Sam's inspection and I watched anxiously for the "black bomber" and Satellite Sam to arrive.

By the time Sam arrived, I had a collection of amateur aircraft mechanics at my side, all with various theories and all anxious to share those theories with the expert from out of town. Sam and I looked over the plane for an hour, maybe two. Satellite Sam and I had a bet regarding which of the local boys had reached the proper conclusion. When I asked Sam, at the end of the inspection, who was right, he replied, "All of them." I said, "Safe answer. You sound like a local." Sam retorted, "I think we will find that with these extremely cold temps, every-thing matters. Look here, the carb heat cable is too short and does not open the flap door all the way; the cross tube in the front of the plane should be in-sulated; the cowling needs to be covered to restrict the airflow, etc. Let's correct those issues and we will take it for a flight to make sure everything is okay. I bet it will run great."

After three hours of tender loving care, the requi-site modifications were made and the flight test underway. To give you the Readers Digest version, the ski plane did not miss a beat.

Sam and I, in turn, poured the blue gas into the "black bomber" and the ski plane respectively, climbed to an altitude of 8500 feet and made pleasant conversation for the duration of our three-hour journey back to Anchorage. The Rainy Pass looked much less ominous from that altitude. To Sam's credit, the ski plane did not miss a beat the entire trip.

As we crossed the Rainy Pass, I safely descended into the Susitna Valley. As I glanced out the pilot's side window, I could see Denali in the distance and Anchorage to the south.

I could not help but think, as I looked to the North and again to the South towards Anchorage, that the mountains were somehow the dividing line between a wild, frozen, unwelcoming and uncivilized place and the more civilized life in Los Anchorage.

I turned my attention to 'aviating, navigating and communicating' as I radioed the tower at the air-port in Anchorage. I requested my landing clearance. The tower said, ". . . you are cleared to land on runway 32; use caution. There is a moose on the runway." In a single breath the dividing line between the civilized and uncivilized had become demonstrably blurred. As I taxied towards the ramp, I took one last picture of the wayward moose being escorted off the runway by our friends from the DOT.

I was still in Alaska, a wild place, to be sure.

CHAPTER 13

Brother Chuck, The Heavenly Nest

IT WAS JUNE IN ALASKA, good to feel warm again. It was primetime for catching Chinook. We were elated by the abundance of fish in the river. As we celebrated on the screen porch, Mr. Sympathy called. I don't think he called with the intent of "roaching my buzz," but it had that effect. I had already planned the summer's guest list, nearly a year in advance. I not only had the guest list planned, with the fishing trips well organized, I had created a schematic showing which guests would be fishing on a given river on a given day.

Mr. Sympathy called to invite himself and a few friends to join us in August. If you are getting the feeling that Mr. Sympathy had a certain amount of leverage over me, go with the feeling. This realization prompted me to gleefully extend an invitation to Mr. Sympathy. "We should be glad to entertain you and your friends for seven days in August," I told him. I had betrayed myself by allowing Mr. Sympathy back into our paradise. God had entrusted me with the key, and I had let Lucifer enter Heaven. Adding insult to injury, Mr. Sympathy was a part of a campaign of whisperers promoting the theme, voices low, "I wonder what he's running from here in Alaska?"

August arrived. Mr. Sympathy unloaded his people. All ten of them. We stacked the Sympathy Clan like cordwood. They were all over the house, in the bunkhouse, in the quarters over the garage. "No worries," said Judas. The solution to the overbooking would be to simply fly the Sympathy Clan, in groups of three Campers at a time, to different rivers in and around the area. Each group could spend the day fishing away from Camp Brewer. We would reverse the process in the evenings, bringing the Campers back in increments of three people at a time. Berta would feed them in stages, as the Campers were phased back into the Camp.

Another means to relieve the over-crowding would be to take two prospective caribou hunters out into the field. Mr. Sympathy had told me that a couple of guys in his group wanted to leave Camp to go hunt for caribou. They would be gone for four or five days. That would lighten the load. We

would take those two souls away from Camp at the earliest possible date, weather permitting.

As luck would have it, bad luck that is, when Mr. Sympathy's crew rolled in, so did the fog and bad weather. There would be no flying on the first day of their trip. The same can be said for day two, three and four of the trip. By day five, I made Jack Nicholson from The Shining look like he was a calm and contented soul. Beyond frustrated, I told the "caribou boys" to put their guns and gear in the plane. We would attempt a flight to the Kvichak River to get them to the Caribou hunting grounds. There was just enough visibility to safely take off.

We departed the Naknek River, taking off down river or to the west, flying towards the Kvichak Bay, which opens up to the Bering Sea. It was my plan to fly over the Naknek River, keeping the river beneath the floats of the plane at all times, with the right bank of the Naknek River in my field of view the entire trip. In the unlikely event forward visibility was reduced, I would keep the right bank of the river in my field of vision at all times. If I lost forward visibility, I would simply reduce power, descend and land on the river. I would complete the entire trip with the right bank of the river in sight. As we flew, although I could land on the river at any time, it was unnerving. As we learned from Tex's accident on the Ugashik River (remember, he hit a shallow spot in the Ugashik and Dick flew into the front of the boat), there are many variables that can make the river impassible, including tides, shallow spots and rocks just under the surface of the water. We traveled twenty or so miles to the mouth of the Naknek River, where the Naknek meets the Kvichak Bay. We turned to the northeast, keeping the bank of the Kvichak Bay off our right wing. The wind was calm, the tide was high. This left us the option of landing in the Kvichak Bay should visibility suddenly go 'zero – zero' or the engine decide it is time to call it quits. We followed the right bank of the Kvichak Bay all the way to the mouth of the Kvichak River, still not having seen anything but the banks of the river and the bay off our right wing. We were just a few minutes away from the proposed landing site. Our forward visibility began to erode. The bank of the Kvichak River tried to play hide and seek. It was time to turn around.

I pulled the power back and extended full flaps to ensure that the radius of the turn was as small as possible. I needed to keep the right side of the river in full view the entirety of the 180-degree turn. The faster the plane is traveling, the larger the radius of the 180-degree turn and the further I am going to be from the shoreline of the river. We slowed to a snail's pace and made a complete 180-degree turn towards home. The bank of the Kvichak River was now off our left wing. The new goal: keep the terra firma off our left wing in sight, with fingers crossed that the visibility would be sufficient so that we would make it back home. It is important for a pilot to have an equal number of take offs and landings in his pilot logbook. We called Camp Brewer on the private air-to-land frequency, "Sitka base, this is Sitka One, how do you read, over?" "Sitka base here, go ahead." "Sitka One is twenty to the Northeast, how is the visibility at base, over?" "Viz is the same as when you departed, we will be down at the dock to greet you, over." We managed an uneventful landing on the Naknek River, some twenty minutes later.

After we landed, I logged that flight in the logbook under a new category called "Never Again."

Berta then relayed the message that my brother, Chuck, had called to see how things were going. Chuck is my oldest brother. It is a strange thing about birth order. An older brother is an older brother. When you have an older brother, he is always your older brother, whether you are eight or fifty-eight. If you're lucky, and I am, his instinct is to look after you, to worry about you, to lecture you. He gives "older brother advice." So, I returned the call to my big brother. He told me he was calling because he was worried his little brother "seemed overwhelmed by such a large group of Campers." There isn't a kinder or more gentle soul in the world than Chuck. He has been giving me advice and counsel, con-

tinuously, for as long as I can remember. You are never alone when you have a brother like Chuck. He wanted to remind me, "You take care of yourself. Don't give away too much of yourself." We then moved on to the subject of flying. I gave him an honest assessment of our trip to the Kvichak River. He said, "I thought you were the one that would never push the weather, with all your years of experience, you are acting like a young pilot." Class dismissed.

My big brother was right. I had succumbed to the pressure. By allowing so many Campers to stay at Camp Brewer, by taking a flight I would later regret, I had allowed Mr. Sympathy, and company, to take too much. It was time for me to make a change, not just in the small picture, but in the big picture. My brother had given his advice in earnest. The following poem was written out of personal frustration. It was written with children as the intended audience to help them to understand that they should not give away too much of themselves. I heard a version of this story in my youth, but not in the form of a poem. I think adults too can benefit from the lesson it hopes to convey. This adult did.

HEAVENLY NEST

From a Heavenly nest — popped two beaks
They just hatched — just three weeks
Soon it's time — to give it a try
Parents must teach — kids to fly

But like God — a father's heart burns
Birds fly off — hope they return

Little Oscar — did his best —
took first flight — returned to nest
Several flights later — Oscar a pro
He can even — outfly a crow

Then one day — Diablo appeared
Holding a worm — properly seared
"A feather for a worm — it's not a sin
Easy to eat — it's a 'win - win'
You'll return home — your tummy so full
Your parents so proud — think you're cool"

Oscar was naive — didn't see horns
The child of God — never felt scorn
Diablo was evil — with bad intent

He didn't care about Oscar — not one cent.
Day after day — even bad weather
Oscar made the trade — worm for feather
His brother warned — "when feathers were small
That did not affect — your flight at all"
"now giving feathers — affects your flight
Brother I tell you — it's not right"

In the future — you'll do your best
With no feathers — can't return to nest
You will have given — so much of your being
It's your nest — you won't be seeing

Giving up small feathers — was no sin
But the big feathers — caused bare skin

Now just — skin and bones
There was no way — to get back home
Birds and heaven — a play with words
Here's a hint — this is not about birds

Ugashik Bob 2018

CHAPTER 14

Love Versus Fear, The Interrogation

As Alaska shut down for the winter season, we turned our attention to skiing, skating and snowmobiles. My girlfriend - I'll call her 'Girly,' because she is - and I had decided to spend a little time in Idaho, another unexpected paradise. Perhaps another story for another day. Like Alaska, we look forward to our time in Idaho with great anticipation. When fall arrives, it signals the need for an extreme exercise program in order to get ready for outdoor winter events. The October, November and December regimen requires a daily routine, alternating daily workouts between plyometrics, running hills, weights, stair climbs and on and on. All this exercise in anticipation of skating, skiing and snowmobiling in Idaho.

We did our part in preparing for the events of winter. Unfortunately, by mid-February, winter had lost what little momentum she had. The skating pond was unsafe to use, the skiing was dismal, even the snowmobile trails were tough to traverse. I woke up in dismay one morning in mid-February with the overwhelming sensation that Mother Nature had let us down, that 'Winter Lied to Me.' With the feeling came a poem:

DEAR GOD - WINTER LIED TO ME

I hate to disparage a season — but Winter lent me a reason,
She lied to me — no place to slide or skate or ski.

So, in the receptacle — winter is tossed,
I wallow in pity — as the season is lost.
With that — from God, a nudge,
Says God — "Winter is not yours to judge.
There's no need to — slander a season."
"But God," I say," — she gave us a reason."

"Winter, she is special to me — not a season to just toss in the sea."
And God suggested — "Make a new wish,
Of times to frolic — to fly, to fish."
Yes — the promise of Spring
We'll drink, we'll laugh — and we'll sing.

Spring is the season of forgiving — carefree, silly, a time for living,
"Dear God, can Winter come to?" — "But, I thought she lied to you?"

"We should forgive winter — forget the grudge."
With that — from God, another nudge,
"Winter is my gift to give and take — I'm glad you forgave her, for my sake.
In closing, "Thank you Lance — for giving winter a second chance."

I thought perhaps I could find other ways to entertain myself, meaning, in Alaska. With Girly's blessing, I made plans for a fishing trip to Alaska. I attempted to contact a young lawyer in my law firm to suggest that we meet at Camp Brewer. We could mix business with pleasure. Although the Naknek River is typically covered in ice in February, I suspected that the unseasonably warm temperatures would cause an early "break-up." In other words, the warm winter would cause the ice to melt early, leaving open water in the area surrounding the Naknek Lake, where the lake meets the Naknek River. If that happens, the rainbow trout fishing can be fantastic. I made a quick call to Harry to see if the river was open and to ask him if he wanted to fish with me. He confirmed that my suspicion was true. It was happening.

Next, I called Racer, because he is the king of spontaneity. Always up for an adventure, Racer readily accepted the invitation. The three of us arrived at the mouth of the river, only to discover that the edge of the boat launch was thirty yards from the open water. I should say that between the edge of the boat launch and the river we found thirty yards of solid ice. The first ten yards was thick ice formed on the shoreline. That ice is formed slowly as the water recedes on the shores of the river. The last twenty yards of ice consists of unpredictable shelf ice. Shelf ice is a thick floating platform of ice that forms on the edge of a river. Although the ice on the shoreline is connected to the shelf ice, from time to time, those thick ice sheets of ice break loose, flowing with the current all the way to the Bering Sea.

Racer is not a fan of shelf ice or cold water. He would only agree to help Harry and I pull the skiff to within ten yards of the edge of the shelf ice. "You boys are on your own after that, you're probably going to die." The three of us, slipping and sliding the entire time, managed to get the skiff within ten feet of the open water, where Racer abandoned ship, so to speak. Harry and I dragged the skiff to the edge of the ice and I climbed into the back of the boat, as we teetered on the edge of the shelf ice. Harry gave the skiff a last heave-ho, and we were floating, or were we? I started the engine, which was whining like a chain saw. That whining sound was the engine's way of telling me that it was not anywhere close to being in the water. But, we had to be on the water since the boat was drifting with the flow of

the current. I could see Racer was getting smaller. As we drifted away, Racer was smiling, waving, then laughing. Apparently, as we pushed the boat off the thick layer of ice, we pushed it onto a slightly submerged layer of shelf ice. I looked down to discover that there must have been a second layer of shelf ice just below the thick layer next to the shoreline. We were sitting on top of a sheet of shelf ice, and the boat was now floating on top of an iceberg. The collective weight of the boat, Harry and I, had caused the ice to break free from the shoreline. The boat and its contents, which included me and Harry, was now floating aimlessly down the river. Harry was quick to grab an oar, in an effort to hammer away at the sheet of ice. One person responded more quickly than Harry, and that was Racer. Before Harry could make his first whack at the ice, Racer yelled from the safety of the shoreline "I told you that you were going to die. That water is so damn cold, I am sure you will have an open casket funeral." Harry beat the ice into submission, we were off the iceberg in no time, the engine happily making power in the river, not whining anymore. But that would not be the end of the whining that day.

As we motored up the river, we dodged various sheets of floating ice and parked the boat 50 yards upstream from another couple of fishermen. With the temperatures being what they were, everyone was well bundled, so it was hard to make out the identity of our fellow anglers. The shelf ice, low water and low tide all contributed to limited space for fishing and fishermen. The open water meant for fishing in a confined area. Clearly, the other fishermen were agitated that we had parked so close to them. But we had little choice in the matter. The winter fishing regulations dictated that we fish between the mouth of Naknek Lake and Trefon's Cabin, which amounted to a few hundred yards of open water. We were sitting in one of a few places open to winter fishing.

The fish gods rewarded Harry with several char and a beautiful rainbow trout. After an uncomfortable amount of time had passed, pride-wise, I finally hooked and landed a respectable char. Seeing me catch a fish, the other group of fishermen started their commentary. "Don't ya'll just hate it when these big city lawyers come to town, fish in OUR spots and catch OUR fish." My 59-year-old self whispered,

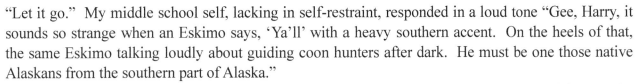

"Let it go." My middle school self, lacking in self-restraint, responded in a loud tone "Gee, Harry, it sounds so strange when an Eskimo says, 'Ya'll' with a heavy southern accent. On the heels of that, the same Eskimo talking loudly about guiding coon hunters after dark. He must be one those native Alaskans from the southern part of Alaska."

Fortunately Harry, always the referee, threw a flag on the play. Harry is also from Louisiana, so he quickly played the role of a peacemaker, yelling, "How is your coon-ass doin'?" The boys made nice. The city slicker lawyer was given a stay of execution.

When we arrived home, Racer asked me if I wanted a glass of white wine. I replied, "Why, are we out of red?" As we sat by the fire, I implored Racer to go fishing with me the next day, but he had a flight in the morning. He asked if the young lawyer from America would arrive in time to go fishing with me in the morning. Fortunately, at that time of year, it remains dark in Alaska until later in the morning. So, fishing the next "morning" means getting going at the crack of noon. I was certain that the fishing would be equally as rewarding the next day. Regretfully, Harry could not join in the fun. He had work to do.

Although the scenery in the winter is not as colorful as the summer, it is surreal to be surrounded by ice and snow while fishing. As I have said before, 'This is a place where you can fish all day, with only your thoughts as company.' Harry was kind enough to assist with the chore of getting the boat down to the water. Surprisingly, there were no other fishermen out that day. The best fishing spot, at the tip of a shoal where the depth of the river dropped precipitously, was the ideal spot to anchor and fish. I figured that the fish would be sitting in schools at the edge of that shoal, in the deepest water. In the course of an hour, the catch included three large char and a single trophy rainbow trout. The decision was made to release the anchor, drifting quietly while fishing in the current of the river.

I was cold and tired, so I sat down in the boat. Surreptitiously, a question arose, "Over the years we have had many conversations about Alaska, the adventures, the beauty and the great fishing here on the Alaska Peninsula, your desire to share time with your family, and more importantly, your son. There have been many conversations about what vexes you. But you never talk about your ex-wife. This is no time for small talk. There are serious questions that need answers. Now, it is said that people who come to Alaska are either running away from something or seeking to find themselves. So, the question arises, what motivated you to come here? Was it something other than your love for Alaska? It has been mentioned a time or two that you might just write a book about Alaska someday. It is intriguing to have heard you explain to various people your reasons for coming to Alaska, your desire to come here. Sure, some people have taken your statement, your reasons, at face-value. But others may question if what you've told them are your real reasons for coming to Alaska."

The diatribe continued, "You may eventually write that book. Since you are going to write about it anyway, let's make a game of it. You're a lawyer. You are a man trained in logic, reason, and evidence. Certainly, you are capable of defending your motivation for coming here." I knew where this was going. I was being challenged to write a legal brief, defending my decision to come to Alaska. Clearly the perception was that I fell into the category of people that came to Alaska because I was "running away from something." Okay… But, for the purpose of this exercise, a brief, not a book, would be in order. A "brief" is prepared by a lawyer who is going into a courtroom to provide the judge with the facts of his case, giving his reasons for the position he is advocating. It was then suggested that, "You may present your legal brief and I will be the judge. Then, a discussion will follow as to the real reasons that you came to Alaska, as if you are presenting a legal argument. Maybe you can use this information as the impetus to write that book or for a portion of the book." I wasn't excited at the prospect of being challenged.

As this exchange took place, the boat continued to drift, now within fifty yards of Trefon's Cabin. Trefon's serves as the Department of Fish and Game's marker for the legal fishing area. Beyond Trefon's Cabin, the fishing is closed. Trefon's Cabin is located at the mouth of the Naknek Lake, where the lake opens up and flows into the Naknek River. It is just one example of a southwestern Alaskan native's log cabin being used as temporary quarters for protection from the elements during winter hunting and trapping, or summer fishing trips. This particular cabin is more simple in its construction, not typical of the work of Trefon, but warm nonetheless.

I thought to myself that I was ready for the debate at that instant. Why delay? I was bold enough to suggest that "Trefon's Cabin is just right there, fifty yards away. Trefon's Cabin it is. No need to delay. I'll fire up the wood stove, complete the debate right now." I think the impression existed that I would require a few days to prepare for the argument, which would take place in California.

Deciding that the debate should take place immediately, I picked up a paddle from the bottom of the boat and slowly maneuvered the boat towards Trefon's Cabin. As I paddled, it was suggested that since the debate would take place in an instant, rules should be established. The rules should model those that lawyers use during the examination of a witness. Yes, rules that are used when conducting a deposition. A deposition occurs before a trial, wherein the plaintiff, the defendant, the lawyers and a court reporter attend the deposition. There is no judge. The deponent, the person being deposed, can be a plaintiff, a defendant, or a third-party witness. The witness is examined under oath. Make no mistake, this process involves adversaries, and the testimony is most frequently used to impeach the witness. But there are times when the parties find that there are areas of common ground, or agreement. These rules were quite readily agreed to.

The interior of Trefon's Cabin was basically a hut with a couple of bunks and a wood stove. As is tradition in Alaska, most such cabins are left open, with survival supplies, matches and wood readily available. Trefon's Cabin was no exception. With the fire blazing, the debate began.

The most effective way for me to communicate the contents of the deposition would be to give you a feel for how the testimony was presented, that is, to put it in a form that is used by judges and lawyers. This is the deposition transcript:

Questioning Lawyer ("QL"): We will start with this premise. You say that you came to Alaska because you wanted to fly airplanes, yes or no?
Me: Yes.

QL: And to fish?
Me: Yes.

QL: To be surrounded by beauty, true?
Me: Certainly.

The questions were purposeful. The tactic was to only ask 'leading' questions - leading me down a path that provided a desired answer. The questions were never open-ended.

QL: It is reported that when Campers wake up at Camp Brewer, the Campers are often greeted on the screen porch with a fire still burning from the night before. One Camper reported seeing guitars, a mandolin and a base guitar left unattended on the porch from the night before, true?

Me: Which question do you want me to answer, the one about the fire still burning unattended or the musical instruments being left on the porch?

QL: Let's start with the fire, still burning, true?
Me: True.

QL: And the musical instruments, just left in the elements?
Me: The porch is covered and enclosed.

QL: Is that a "yes?"
Me: Yes.

QL: Is there alcohol involved?
Me: That's just the boys, blowing off steam.

QL: Is that a "Yes?"
Me: Yes.

QL: You boys ever have any "ladies" at the house?

Me: Does that include "Berta?"

QL: I'll ask the questions.
Me: Never. Well, not like you are inferring - not like that, anyway.

QL: I hear a lot of talk about one "Sarah," who was Sarah?
Me: Sarah was my dog. We talk about her as if she is human, because she practically was.

QL: Sounds, plausible. And you say that you built the house on the Naknek River so that you could share time here with your family, true or false?
Me: True.

QL: But the overriding reason, you have said, is that you wanted to share time with your son, right?
Me: Absolutely.

I no longer have command of the discussion. The interrogation, not all of which is included here, has lasted for twenty relentless minutes. I sit, armpits generating moisture, hoping nervously for a mistake.

QL: But you struggled in your marriage, didn't you?
Me: Yes.

QL: So, you are in the class of people that came to Alaska because you are running away from something, true or false?
Me: It's False. The statement is False.

I am outside my comfort zone with this line of questioning. But, a mistake is about to be made, the door will be opened for me.

QL: If fear didn't make you come to Alaska, if you were not running away from your marriage, then why? What motivated you come to Alaska?

Excellent, the open-ended question. Thank You.

Me: People, including myself, are either motivated by love or fear. I was motivated by love, not fear. Allow me to provide context. When I was in my first year of college, I took a class, "Introduction to Psychology- Psych: 101." One lesson, that I will never forget, became the lesson to live by. The professor presented us with the theory that humans are either motivated by love or fear. All of life's decisions, everything that motivates us, can be broken down to a decision that is driven by love or fear. The love versus fear dilemma applies to everything from our decision on whether or not to fly in an airplane; to the decision about whether to get involved in a love relationship; the decision of whether to hike to a bear-infested fishing hole; to the decision on whether or not to quit drinking alcohol or using drugs. Every decision we make is driven by our love for something or someone or our fear of something or someone. It was a simple concept that I took with me when I left college. As I have walked through life, at each fork in the road, each time a difficult decision had to be made, I asked myself, "Is your decision motivated by love or fear?" Over time, I learned that I should make every effort to make my decisions based upon my love for something, to let love drive the desire to move towards something or someone. I should avoid making any decision on the basis of fear of an outcome or fear of a person's response to my decision.

QL: So, you admit that you came to Alaska because of fear, because you were running away, isn't that true?
Me: It's False.

QL: What's false about that statement?
Me: One could take the view that I ran away to Alaska out of fear, in an effort to escape not-so-happy times in America. On the other hand, if you believe the answer I gave to the last question, that love became my motivating factor, you might take the position that I came here because it would be an opportunity to demonstrate to my son, to friends, to family, that there is more to life than the day-to-day grind of the city. There are lessons to be learned, opportunities to teach; experiences to be had; stories to be shared. There is epic scenery, so surreal that after returning to America for ten minutes you would

swear that everything you witnessed during your time in Alaska was a movie you watched, not something you actually did. And the wildlife. You can stand fifty yards from fighting bears, watching them battle for fish right in front of you. Perhaps a wolf will show up on a river to display his superior ability to catch fish; or an eagle will soar over your head, surprising you with a dive bomb right in front of you to grab an oversized char from the river; maybe two juvenile foxes,

siblings, will conduct their fight practice or rehearse their fighting skills right out the front window. And then there's the fishing. I wish I had a dime for every time I have heard a Camper say, "This is the biggest fish I have ever caught, never mind caught, seen." Or "I have never caught so many fish in my life." "This is the best trip of my life." "This may be the best day of my life." Or a non-fisherman Camper say: "I never thought I would be this close to a bear." "I have never seen an eagle in the wild before." "I have never seen a whale before." The spontaneous declarations are endless. And there are the teaching moments. It is hard to teach a young boy how to start a fire with wet wood in Newport Beach; how to repair a carburetor on a boat motor; how to make peace with a bear that is thirty yards away; the best way to handle a four-wheeler in deep sand or snow; how to conduct yourself when your friend catches six fish, while you catch none; the proper way to humanely release a fish; why and when it is appropriate for a man to kill an animal; the importance of hunting to people who count on hunting, not a supermarket, as a source for food. Should I continue?

QL: You believe that this place, Alaska, your place, has had that effect?
Me: Which place? My place, or Alaska?

QL: Don't be coy, just answer the question.
Me: Yes, I do. And I have evidence. I can call many, many people to the witness stand. They will substantiate what I am saying. They will bring demonstrative evidence, not just stories, but pictures.
The questioning went on – extensively – for an hour. I am going to summarize the remainder of

the deposition because the process of writing about it in its entirety would take several hours. In fact, I could fill an entire book containing my responses to questions with regard to the beauty of Alaska, about the extraordinary people I have met, the experiences we have had flying and fishing, and the lessons we have learned from our experiences. My friends in Alaska are some of the people that I'm closest to in this world. So much so that when they leave this party, I will probably wish that I could go too.

Towards the end of the deposition, the voice I was hearing, which sounded a lot like my own voice, seemed to be moved by what I was saying. At the outset, I am not sure that the voice believed that the events and experiences I was describing actually could take place outside the fantasy of a movie theatre, or the internet, or a game-boy or computer. I believe my testimony had shaken him. In the end, I heard the voice say, "Technology has overwhelmed this generation of people. It would be wonderful if more people from this generation could touch and feel nature, be in Alaska. Before my last question I want to say that there never has been an age nor a time in the history of man that the experiences you have described were more needed than they are today." The voice had one final question.

QL: Do you understand the significance of the events that you have described – that you have experienced--- in Alaska?
Me: I do.

The fire in the wood stove had slowly lost its energy, as did I. I dozed off for a bit. When I awoke with the chill in the air, the boat was covered in a couple of inches of snow. Time for me to head back to the warmth of Camp Brewer, maybe to write one last poem to give life to the events of the day.

LOVE VERSUS FEAR

Jesse took off his baseball mitt — there he placed —
a big ole' spit
"I'm not going to the game tonight — Nolan's pitch-
ing — filled with fright"

His brother teased — what about Sarah Macrity
Her eyes on you — she's quite pretty

"I can't hit — Nolan's curve ball
And Sarah — she's so tall
I'm not sure — how to talk
After striking out — it's a long walk."

The age-old question — through the years
What will win — love or fears
Life's decisions — this conflict
Love or fear — hard to pick

Many years passed — Jesse's new life
The big city lawyer — called his wife
Sarah asked — "why the strife
Talk to me — love of my life"
Jesse explained — the new case
A white collar crime — the criminal's face
Sarah suggested — short of tears
"It all comes down — to love versus fears"

He feared — she can't admire
The allegations — his client conspired
Loved -helping his kids — pay for school
Feared -his colleague's — ridicule
Loved -helping — client make bail
Feared -good man — ends up in jail

Sarah understood him — his generous heart
"Let's go back — from where we start
Love dictates — decisions of the past
Love provides — a joy that lasts"

It all comes down to love versus fear.

THE END